JAMES W. MOORE

There's a H●le in Your Soul That Only God Can Fill

DIMENSIONS
FOR LIVING
NASHVILLE

THERE'S A HOLE IN YOUR SOUL THAT ONLY GOD CAN FILL

This book is printed on acid-free paper.

Library of Congress Cataloging-in-Publication Data

Moore, James W. (James Wendell), 1938-
   There's a hole in your soul that only God can fill / James W. Moore.
      p. cm.
   ISBN 0-687-05456-7 (pbk. : alk. paper)
   1. Christian life—Methodist authors.   I. Title.
   BY4501.3.M6646 2005
   248.4—dc22

2005008638

All scripture quotations, unless noted otherwise, are taken from the *New Revised Standard Version of the Bible,* copyright 1989, by the Division of Christian Education of the National Council of the Churches of Christ in the United States of America. Used by permission. All rights reserved.

ISBN-13: 978-0-687-05456-5

07 08 09 10 11 12 13 14—10 9 8 7 6 5 4 3
MANUFACTURED IN THE UNITED STATES OF AMERICA

For G.G.

CONTENTS

Introduction—"My Soul Is Restless, O God, 'Til It
   Finds Its Rest in Thee" 7

1. Faith in God—"Got My Own" 15

2. Trust in God—"Have You Ever Run Out of Gas?" 23

3. Excitement in God—"I've Got a Strong Case of the
   'Can't Help Its' ". 31

4. Disciples of God—"Dear Hope, Keep Living Up to
   Your Name" 39

5. Christlikeness in God—"Have No Regrets" 47

6. Eternal Life in God—"What Do We Believe About
   Eternal Life?" 57

7. Sharing God with Children—"Train Up a Child" 65

8. Finding God in the Bible—"How to Read and
   Understand the Bible". 75

9. Loyalty to God and the Church—"Hold On to the
   Church with Both Hands" 81

10. New Life in God—"What Do You Want Me to Do
    Now?". 89

11. Commitment to God—"Be Careful What You Lean
    Your Weight On". 97

12. The Song of God—"God Gave the Song" 105

13. Bringing Others to God—"He Couldn't Keep Jesus to Himself" 113

14. Marriage and God—"Celebrating the Gift of Marriage" 121

15. Purpose in God—"The Power of a Purpose" 129

Suggestions for Leading a Study 137

INTRODUCTION

"My Soul Is Restless, O God, 'Til It Finds Its Rest in Thee"

Scripture: Colossians 3:1-4

Some time ago while I was on a speaking engagement in another city, a highly successful businessman invited me to stop by his office for lunch. He proudly showed me around his elegant and luxurious business suite, and we ended up in his beautifully appointed private office. He closed the door, sat down, and rather abruptly he said, "Jim, I wanted to talk with you because I am absolutely miserable. I have everything, but I have nothing. I have a wonderful family, an expensive home, three luxury cars, a lake house, a good business, a respected profession, and I'm in good health. Who could want more? I have everything I've always dreamed of having, and more; and yet, I feel so empty inside. The truth is, I'm bored to tears!" Here in this man's candid confession we see it dramatically: a graphic picture of the deadly disease of boredom.

God never meant life to be boring. Christ came to bring us abundant life. He came to show us how to live life to the full, how to live zestfully. And yet it is a sad fact that many people today are spiritually tired, emotionally worn, and miserably bored.

J. Wallace Hamilton, in his book *Serendipity,* reminds us of that thought-provoking comment by a noted London physician. The doctor, speaking to a minister friend, said, "After all, the most deadly of human diseases is one which we cannot touch with a knife or save people from with drugs."

"You mean cancer?" the minister asked.

"Oh no. We'll get that little devil yet. I mean boredom! There is more real wretchedness, more torment driving folks to folly, or what you parsons call sin, due to boredom than to anything else. Men and women will do almost anything to escape it. They will drink, drug themselves, sell their bodies and their souls, fling themselves into crazy fads. They will torture themselves and other people to escape the misery of being bored. Anyone who discovers the cure for that will put an end to more human tragedy than can all of us doctors put together" (J. Wallace Hamilton, *Serendipity,* Westwood, N.J.: Fleming H. Revell Co., 1965, pp. 51-52).

The deadly disease of boredom, that's what the doctor was talking about; a disease that leads directly to more disruption of lives and more destruction than we can imagine.

Many a marriage problem is the symptom of the deeper problem of boredom, the consequence of a relationship grown stale and monotonous. Somehow, the courtship stops and the marriage withers. The couple begins taking each other for granted, and boredom sets in. This is a chief cause of unfaithfulness in marriage. Boredom creeps in and marriage partners seek excitement elsewhere.

A middle-aged man was talking with a counselor once about his relationship with his wife. The counselor encouraged the man to "continue the courtship," to be creative and enthusiastic and thoughtful, to work at courting his wife; and the man said, "What's the use of chasing the bus after you've already caught it?"

And that man wonders why his marriage is in trouble! He has a lot to learn about love and "love making." His marriage was about to break up and "go under" due to laziness and selfishness and boredom.

Many young people get in trouble by doing foolish, dangerous things because they feel bored and long for excitement. It's true not just today, but in every generation. In every generation some young people go over the edge looking for a thrill. They steal hubcaps or break into a store or experiment with sex or get drunk or pack a gun or play around with drugs or play "chicken" in a speeding car. Why? Is it because they are bad? No, it's because they are bored; they're in a frantic search for excitement, trying to fill the vacuum, the emptiness within.

Remember that classic movie of the 1950s *Rebel Without a Cause*? James Dean starred in that film, playing the role of an anguished teenage rebel, a rebel without a cause, a rebel who was simply bored, fed up, world-weary, having everything but a purpose, everything but a reason for living.

Many emotional problems (all the way from melancholy to deep depression) may well be rooted in boredom. Let me give just one example, a new sociological problem that has just popped up in recent years: the runaway mom!

For years we have seen dads in our society running away from the pressures and responsibilities of the home. But in recent decades the "runaway mom" has surfaced. We saw it in the hit movie *Kramer vs. Kramer,* in which the mom (played by Meryl Streep) stresses out and feels she has to get away, leaving the dad (played by Dustin Hoffman) and her young son behind as she goes away to "find herself."

The "runaway mom," overwhelmed by the demands of being on call twenty-four hours a day, seven days a week as a wife and mother and feeling that life is somehow passing her by, leaves a note saying, "I love you, but I can't take it anymore." And then while her child is in school and her husband is at work, she vanishes. She runs away because she feels stressed to the max, and at the same time, she feels unappreciated, unfulfilled—and bored to tears with her unromantic life. Over and over again we see it, the deadly disease of boredom and what it can do to us.

Now, I bring this up because I am absolutely convinced that life does not have to be boring or monotonous or routine, futile or wearisome. I believe with all my heart that God meant life to be joyous and creative, zestful and meaningful, exciting and full! You see, we don't have to give in to boredom. We don't have to be infected with that debilitating disease. But the question is, what is the antidote? What is the miracle cure? How do we fight off the temptation to throw in the towel and quit on life? How do we find this abundant life that Jesus talked about? What is the Christian solution to the destructive forces of boredom?

Let me list a few ideas for us to think about together. I'm sure you will think of others.

First of All, Recognize Boredom for What It Really Is

You see, boredom is not so much the problem as it is a symptom of a much deeper problem. Boredom is a symptom of emptiness, the inner emptiness that comes from loving or craving the wrong things, temporal things that will never satisfy; and then when we get them, they don't measure up, they don't fill the vacuum, they rust, they break, they de-value, and we feel cheated, short-changed, empty, let-down, and bored to tears.

The apostle Paul tried to warn us about this. He said, "Set your minds on things that are above" (Colossians 3:2), on things that last, on the divine, the eternal, on God, not on earthly things.

Jesus said it too. He said, "Strive first for the kingdom of God" (Matthew 6:33). Put that first, and everything else will fall into place for you.

Both the Old and New Testaments tell us boldly to love God with all your heart (see Deuteronomy 6:4-5, Leviticus 19:18, Matthew 22:34-40, and Luke 10:25-28).

You see, there is a special space in our hearts that only God can fill. Our souls are wired up so that they just cannot be happy with anything less than God. Augustine put it like this: "Our souls are restless until they find their rest in Thee."

The point is clear: When we set our affections on things below, we come up empty and dissatisfied and depressed and bored. J. Wallace Hamilton sums it up for us like this:

> Love the Lord thy God with all thy heart ... (Matthew 22:37). And such is the nature of the human heart.... It must love something. Its hungers must be fed as the hungers of the body [must be fed]; the affections must be set on something. The strong feelings must have something to lay hold upon, to wrap themselves around, or lacking [that], leave a hunger as painful in the soul as hunger in the body when it has no solid food. Here then ... is the torment of boredom: an emptiness in the soul, a basic human need

unanswered, an unfed craving of the heart for some devotion to give life glory and meaning ... [and] zest....

The bored people are not the busy people. They are the empty people, whether busy or not, people with nothing to live for and nothing outside themselves to fix [their] affections upon—the "hollow [people]" T. S. Eliot talked about, for whom life is void of meaning. Boredom is just another name for emptiness. (*Serendipity*, pp. 52-53)

I had a speech teacher in college who liked to say, "Don't put the em-PHA-sis on the wrong syl-LAB-le!"

Many people today find their lives coming up empty because they are emphasizing the wrong syllables. If you and I give our major emphasis, our major affection, our major commitment to anything less than God, then we will eventually end up restless and dissatisfied because there is a hole in our souls that only God can fill!

First of all, we need to recognize boredom for what it really is—a symptom of emptiness, a red flag that we have drifted away from God, a reminder that our souls are restless apart from God.

Second, See Time as a Precious Gift from God

Not long ago I stepped on an elevator at Methodist Hospital. Already on board was a handsome elderly gentleman who looked to be in his nineties. I spoke to him and said, "Isn't this a beautiful day?" With a chuckle, the man answered, "Well, Sonny, when you get over ninety like me, and you wake up and open your eyes and realize you're still alive, every day is a beautiful day!"

But, you see, as Christians we don't have to wait around until we are ninety years old to feel that way. For the Christian, every day is a beautiful day because we see every moment of every day as a precious gift from God.

Some years ago, some teenage boys decided to skip Sunday school. While a thousand people were in their Sunday school classes studying the lesson of the day, these teenage boys thought it would be funny to pull the red fire alarm lever on the wall in one of the church buildings.

The alarm went off, extremely loudly, and Sunday school was disrupted. Most people filed out in an orderly fashion, but some of the older people went into panic mode and tried to move too fast. One elderly man fell on the stairs, but fortunately a young couple caught him and prevented what could have been a very serious injury. Another man's heart began to race and a woman had to be treated for high blood pressure. Both were rushed to the hospital.

After it was all over, the youth director brought the teenage boys to my office. They confessed what they had done. They explained that they had no idea that their little prank would cause such a commotion. They apologized and asked for forgiveness and received it.

Then almost as an afterthought, one of them said, "We didn't mean any harm. We were bored and had nothing else to do. We were just 'killing time.'" Now, that's a common phrase, "killing time," but if we stop to think about it, that's a troublesome thing to say. It should make us shudder within. What could be more wasteful?

As Christians, we see time as a precious and valuable gift from God to be used wisely and creatively and constructively. I saw a bumper sticker recently that expressed this well. It read: "Today Is God's Gift to Us; That's Why We Call It the Present."

That's our calling as Christians, to see every day as a new opportunity to serve God and love people in a fresh, unique way that will never come again. The psalmist put it like this: "This is the day that the LORD has made; let us rejoice and be glad in it" (Psalm 118:24).

Third and Finally, Another Antidote to the Disease of Boredom Is to Get Outside Yourself

The truth is that self-centeredness is one of the chief causes of boredom. A selfish person can possess every comfort and luxury available to humankind and yet still be cynical and bitter and miserable and bored. This is one of the main themes of F. Scott Fitzgerald's book *The Great Gatsby,* how the spoiled and selfish super-rich can also be bored to tears.

If you want to have a zestful and joyous life, the key is to get outside yourself; forget yourself and reach out in love to other people. This is especially and uniquely true when we reach out to others in the spirit of Jesus Christ.

During a lecture on mental health, Dr. Karl Menninger was asked an interesting question: "Dr. Menninger, if you felt you were coming apart emotionally and were headed for a nervous breakdown, what would you do?"

The inquirer expected the great psychiatrist to say that in that situation he would go to a psychiatrist, but Dr. Menninger surprised him with his answer. He said, "I would go straight to the front door, turn the knob, cross the tracks, and find somebody who needs me, and I would help them. That's what I would do." Karl Menninger is a smart man. He knows how important it is to get outside yourself and reach out in love to others in the name of God and in the spirit of Christ.

Let me sum up. First, recognize boredom for what it really is, the symptom of emptiness. Second, see time as a precious gift from God. And third, in the name of God, get outside yourself.

Now, let me conclude with this: The real key to dealing with the problem of boredom is to see life as partnership with God. What could be more exciting than that? What could be more exhilarating than that? What could be more thrilling than that? Seeing life as a sacred partnership with God, doing everything we do as if we were doing it for God.

Some years ago, Dag Hammarskjöld said it beautifully in a prayer: "Give me a pure heart—that I may see Thee, / A humble heart—that I may hear Thee, / A heart of love—that I may serve Thee, / A heart of faith—that I may abide in Thee" (*Markings,* New York: Knopf, 1964).

On the one hand, when we live centered in God, seeking to serve him, trying our best to do his will, daily celebrating his presence with us and his amazing grace toward us, then life can be full and joyful and exhilarating. On the other hand, when we neglect God or ignore God or turn away from God, the result is boredom or emptiness because there is a hole in our souls that only God can fill.

In this book, we will take a look at the crucial importance of faith in God, trust in God, commitment to God, purpose in God and other matters of dramatic significance in the spiritual life because apart from these, or without these... *There's a Hole in Your Soul that Only God Can Fill.*

1. FAITH IN GOD

"Got My Own"

Scripture: Philippians 2:12-13

A year or so ago, I was driving through the streets of Houston with our grandson Paul. Paul was six years old at the time. He noticed a small metal canister on the front seat beside me, and he asked me, "Gran, what's in that little can?" I said, "Those are cinnamon-flavored mints. They are called Altoids." Paul said, "I wonder how they taste."

Well, I wasn't born yesterday, so I got the not-so-subtle hint and asked him, "Would you like to try one? They are a little strong, but you can give them a try if you like."

Paul tried them, and he liked them. He liked them a lot. So over the next days and months, sharing cinnamon-flavored Altoids became "our thing." Grandson and Granddad sharing Altoids. Every time we were together, Paul would say, "Gran, do you have any Altoids today?" Well, of course I realized how important this "Altoids bonding" between the two of us had become, so I always made sure to have cinnamon-flavored Altoids in my possession to share with Paul.

This became such a staple of our relationship that Paul's mother, my daughter Jodi, told me that one day their family was walking through a large shopping mall in Dallas and as they passed a bakery where cinnamon rolls were baking, Paul said, "It smells like Gran is around here!"

Last summer a friend of ours got married in a church in Dallas, and our whole family went together to the wedding. We were all sitting together on the same long pew. Our granddaughter Sarah was on the aisle so she could see the bride up close as the bride came down the aisle, and Paul was next to me in the center of the pew.

During the prelude, I looked over at Paul, so handsome dressed up in his navy blue blazer, khaki slacks, white dress shirt, and plaid bow tie, with his feet not touching the floor, just dangling off the pew; and I whispered to Paul, "Paul, do you want an Altoid?"

Paul looked at me, smiled, and pointed to the right-side pocket of his khaki slacks. I could see the shape of a small canister in his pocket. He tapped it with his fingers and said proudly, "Got my own!" I thought to myself, *Paul is growing up*. The Saturday before Christmas, Paul called June (my wife, Paul's grand-mother) and me on the phone. He told us that he was in the car with his mother, and they were going Christmas shopping. He told us he was working on his shopping list, and he wanted to know what we would like for him to give us for Christmas. We both said, "Oh, Paul, if you will just come to see us for Christmas, that's all the present we need. That would be the best Christmas present you could give us!"

Paul replied, "Well, I am coming to see you, but I'd kind of like to buy you something." He paused for a minute, and then he said, "Mimi and Gran, I like to be thoughtful!"

When he said that, somewhere in heaven God was smiling, and I realized again, *Paul is growing up*. We said, "Paul, you just pick out something you think we would like."

Then at Christmas, when our family got together to open our gifts, there was a lot of fun and excitement during the gift-opening. Paul gave June a piece of jewelry, a beautiful necklace, and said, "Mimi, I know you like jewelry." And then, I saw it under the tree, a small gift that looked like it had been wrapped by a six-year-old boy. It had as much adhesive tape on it as paper, and it had my name on it in bold, first-grade letters.

I was excited to see it, but not nearly as excited as Paul was. He grabbed the gift and brought it over to me. He was beaming, so happy to give me the gift he had thoughtfully and lovingly picked out just for me. He stood right in front of me to watch me open it. "You're going to love it, Gran! You're going to love it!" Paul said.

I tore into the package, and what do you think it was? That's right: a small canister of cinnamon-flavored Altoids! I'll never forget the look on Paul's face—which, by the way, I saw through tears of joy. He was so excited and so proud of what he had done. I remembered that wonderful Bible verse, "It is more blessed to give than to receive," and I saw the joy of that in Paul's face.

I said, "Paul, thank you so much. This is just what I wanted!" and I hugged him. He hugged me back and said, "I *knew* you would like that. That's why I picked it out for you!"

Now, Paul had had a look of delight earlier in the evening when he opened his "Game Boy Advance," but this was different; just six years old, and he had discovered and celebrated the joy of being thoughtful, the joy of giving. And once again I thought to myself, *Paul is growing up.*

First, I shared with him . . .
then, he got his own . . .
and finally, he shared with others.

Well, you may be wondering, *What in the world does this have to do with the Christian faith?*

Well, actually a whole lot, because that's precisely how it works in the world of faith. Someone shares his or her faith with us. Then, we get our own faith. And finally, we share our faith, our hope, and our love with others.

This is what the passage in Philippians 2 is about. Paul is writing to his dear Philippian friends. He was so close to them. He loved them deeply, and they loved him. It's interesting to note that this was the only church Paul would accept gifts from. He could accept gifts from them because he had such a close and warm relationship with them. He knew that they trusted him completely and that they would never ever be suspicious of him. They were like his very own children, and he was their father figure. Paul had taught them the faith, he had nourished them and advised them and encouraged them, and they were so dependent upon him and his leadership and his counsel. And therein was the problem, because Paul knew that his days on earth were numbered. He knew that soon he would be executed by the Romans, that he no longer would be around to "parent" them in the faith, that soon now (very soon) they would have to grow up and stand on their own two feet spiritually. And so he said to them, in essence, "I'm not going to be around much longer to spoon-feed you, so you're going to have to work out your own salvation. In other words, grow up! Stand tall! Be strong! Be mature! Take responsibility now for your own spiritual life. Find your own faith, hope, and love. I won't be with you, but God will. God will be with you every step of the way, and he will see you through. I have shared my faith with you. Now it's time for you to grow up and get your own faith, so that you can share your faith with others."

Let me ask you something: When it comes to faith, can you say, "Got my own!"? When it comes to hope, can you say, "Got my own!"? When it comes to love, can you say, "Got my own!"?

Let's take a look at these three dramatic signs of spiritual maturity and see how we are doing in each category.

First, We Need Our Own Faith

Remember with me the old story about the little boy who was asked why he was a Christian. He answered, "I don't know for sure, but I think it runs in our family!"

That's a cute story, isn't it? But we need hurriedly to add a footnote, and the footnote is this: We can ride on the coattails of our family for just so long, and then each one of us individually has to make his or her own personal decision for Jesus Christ.

The family can help us here and there, and it's great when they do; but each of us at some point has to make that personal decision to receive Christ into his or her own heart.

It's terrific when Granddad is a devoted Christian. It's wonderful when Mom is a committed disciple. It's fantastic if Dad is a consecrated and active churchman. But somewhere along the way, I have to make my own decision, my own commitment, my own acceptance of Christ as my personal Savior and Lord.

Have you made that decision yet? Have you invited Christ into your life? Have you turned your life over to him?

Some years ago in Los Angeles, a sixteen-year-old girl made a mistake and consequently realized that she was expecting a child.

She was terrified. Her mother was a devout Christian, and the young girl couldn't figure out how to tell her mother. She was embarrassed, ashamed, and scared to death. She had a big problem, and she didn't know what to do.

That sixteen-year-old girl decided that her life was over, so she boarded a bus to go to a place to end it all, but as she was on the bus, she heard a voice—clear as a bell—saying, *"Don't do this!"* She looked around, but no one on the bus had spoken. The bus was nearly empty. One passenger was asleep, and the other two were reading, and the voice had not come from their direction anyway. Then she heard it again: *"Don't do this!"*

The girl then got off the bus and went home. She told her mother everything. Her mom was great. Her mother held her and loved her, and then her mother said, "You know who that voice on the bus was, don't you? That was Jesus. He has a special plan for your baby."

Eight months later, the young girl gave birth to a baby boy, and God did have a special plan for that baby. He grew up to be a minister, and today he is the senior pastor of one of the largest, most effective and most influential churches in America.

When that minister tells the story of how the voice of Jesus saved him and his mother, he ends by quoting the hymn:

I love to tell the story
of unseen things above,
of Jesus and his glory,
of Jesus and his love.

I love to tell the story,
because I know 'tis true;
it satisfies my longings
as nothing else can do.

I love to tell the story,
'twill be my theme in glory,
to tell the old, old story
of Jesus and his love.
("I Love to Tell the Story," Katherine Hankey, 1868)

And then that minister says, Jesus saved me. He saved my life. If it weren't for Him I wouldn't be here.

In a different way, in a less dramatic way, I can say that too. Not in the way that that great minister describes, but in a deeply spiritual way, I can say that, too.

Jesus saved me.
He turned my life around.
He breathed new life into me
and if it were not for him,
I would not be here
standing in this pulpit today.

Can you say that? Can you? Have you personally accepted Jesus Christ as the Lord and Savior of your life? Have you committed your heart, your soul, your life to him?

When it comes to faith, can you say, "Got my own!"?

We need, first of all, our own personal faith.

Second, We Need Our Own Hope

A woman was at work one day when she received a phone call telling her that her daughter was very sick with a high fever. The woman left work immediately and stopped by the pharmacy to get some medication for her daughter.

When she came out of the drug store, however, the woman discovered that in her concern and haste she had locked her keys in the car. She was now close to panic. She needed to get into the car and get home with the medicine fast, but now she was locked out of her car. What on earth was she going to do?

The woman remembered hearing about people using a wire coat hanger to open the door. She found one on the ground nearby and tried her best to use it to get into the car, but no luck. She didn't know how to do that.

In desperation now, she prayed, "O God, please send someone to help me!"

A few minutes later an old car pulled up, and a rough-looking character got out. The woman thought, *O Lord,* this *is who you sent to help me?*

The man walked over to her and said, "Looks like you need a little assistance. Can I help you?"

"Oh yes," the woman said. "My daughter is very sick. I stopped to get her some medicine, and I locked my keys in the car. I must get home to her. Please, can you use this hanger to unlock my car?"

"Sure," the man said. He took the hanger, and in less than a minute, the car was opened. The woman hugged the man and said, "Thank you so much! You are a very nice man."

The man replied, "Some people don't think I'm so nice. I just got out of prison yesterday. I was in prison for car theft."

The woman hugged the man again, and with sobbing tears, she cried out loud, "Oh, thank you, God! You even sent a professional!"

This story is a parable for us. It reminds us that God doesn't always send us what we expect, but he will always send us what we need. It's up to us to have the wisdom to recognize the difference and to be thankful.

This is why we as Christians are people of hope, because we know that even though we will have difficulties and setbacks in this life, ultimately nothing can defeat us. God wins, and he wants to share his victory with us. This is God's promise, to always be with us and to eventually see us through. That is our hope. Even if a victory does not come for us in this life, it will come in the life to come.

But let me ask you, when it comes to hope, can you say, "Got my own!"?

Third and Finally, We Need Our Own Love

Jesus taught us in words and deeds the miracle of love, but the question is, have we really learned the lesson of love yet?

It was a beautiful spring day. A mother, a father, and their little girl were out in the family car for a ride. The weather was so gorgeous that they rolled down the windows to enjoy the breezes and fragrances of the springtime.

Suddenly, a large bee darted into the car and started buzzing around. The little girl went into a panic because she was highly allergic to bee stings. If she were stung, she could die within the hour.

"Oh, Daddy!" she squealed in horror. "It's a bee! It's going to sting me!"

The father pulled the car to a stop and reached back to try to catch the bee. Buzzing around toward him, the bee bumped against the front windshield. There the father trapped the bee in his fist.

Holding it in his closed hand, the father waited for the inevitable sting. The bee stung the father's hand, and in pain, the father let go of the bee, and the bee was loose in the car again. The little girl again panicked, "Daddy, it's going to sting me!"

The father said gently, "No, honey, he's not going to sting you now. Look at my hand. The bee's stinger is in my hand, and he can't hurt you now."

The father let the bee sting him to save his daughter's life.

Jesus took the sting of death on the cross, and through his sacrificial love he saved us. And in that incredible act of self-giving, he taught us not only how much he loves us, but also how he wants us to love one another.

Jesus loves us sacrificially, generously, graciously, unconditionally—and that's how he wants us to love.

Can you love like that? *Do* you love like that? *Will* you love like that?

Let me ask you something: When it comes to faith, hope, and love, can you say, "Got my own!"?

2. TRUST IN GOD

"Have You Ever Run Out of Gas?"

Scripture: Philippians 3:12-16

A few years ago, an interesting thing happened during the Rose Bowl Parade on New Year's Day. With thousands watching in person along the parade route and millions more watching on television, the world-famous Tournament of Roses Parade suddenly ground to a halt. There was a long delay because one of the large floats lost power and coasted to a complete stop. The beautiful float was so huge that it covered most of the street, and the other floats and the marching bands could not get around it, so the parade was stopped for some time.

A quick investigation revealed that the problem was not some major mechanical failure that had stopped the float and delayed the whole parade. No, the problem was really very elementary. The large, expensive float, in all of its floral splendor, had quite simply run out of gas very near the place where it had started. Someone had to run and find a gallon of gas before the Tournament of Roses Parade could start up again!

But then there is the rest of the story, which is most ironic, for you see, the float that ran out of gas that day was being sponsored by one of the largest and most successful oil and gas companies in the world! How embarrassing! There were some red faces along the parade route and back at the petroleum company's home office.

But, you know, we've all had that problem, haven't we? We've all had the experience of running out of gas. With some of us drivers, it's because we simply forget to watch the fuel gauge on the car's dashboard.

With men in particular, it's often even more complicated, because not only do men sometimes forget to watch the fuel gauge, but in addition, men just don't like to stop! When we men get behind the wheel, we think we are in the Indianapolis 500 and that stopping is a headache, a distraction, and a waste of time. We men drivers think we have to hurry up and get there; we have to get ahead of that 18-wheeler; we have to beat the time we made on our last trip. So, we don't want to stop for a time-consuming thing like putting gas in the tank. We don't want to take the time to stop for anything! And so, sometimes we push it too close, and we sputter and come to a complete stop, because when the fuel is gone, it's gone! When the fuel is gone, the car stops.

Now, the point is, it can happen to any of us. If we don't pay attention, we can run out of gas! This is also true spiritually. If we are not careful, if we are not intentional, if we don't pay attention, we can run out of gas spiritually.

This is precisely what the apostle Paul was talking about in his letter to the Philippians. Paul was in prison at the time he wrote this letter. Many scholars believe that Paul was executed by the Romans not long after he sent this letter. He probably saw the handwriting on the wall. He likely knew that his days on earth were quickly coming to a close, so he wrote to his good friends in the Philippian church to affirm them, to assure them, to give them his last words of affection and instruction, and to encourage them to hang in there, to hold on to their faith, and not to "run out of gas" when he was no longer around to watch over them and to feed them spiritually.

Paul expressed it like this: "Forgetting what lies behind and straining forward to what lies ahead, I press on toward the goal for the prize of the heavenly call of God in Christ Jesus. Let those of us then who are mature be of the same mind. . . . Only let us hold fast to what we have attained" (Philippians 3:13*b*-16).

In other words, Paul was saying to them, "Hold on to your faith, come what may. Whatever happens, don't lose heart! Keep on believing! Keep on trusting God! Keep on growing spiritually. Don't give up! Don't quit! Don't run out of gas! Press on!"

Have you heard about the convention where the corporate sales manager got up before all 2,000 of the firm's salespersons and asked, "Did the Wright brothers ever quit?" The members of the sales force shouted, "No!" Then the manager yelled out, "Did

Charles Lindbergh ever quit?" Again, the salespersons shouted back, "No!" A third time the manager yelled out: "Did Joan of Arc ever quit?" The salespeople, warming to the moment, shouted back even louder, "No!" This questioning and answering continued, and then the sales manager bellowed out one last time: "Did Thorndyke McKeester ever quit?" There was a long silence. Finally, one brave man stood up and said what everybody else was thinking. "Sir, forgive me for asking, but who is Thorndyke McKeester? We never heard of him." The sales manager snapped back, "Of course you never heard of him, because he quit!"

Now, let me say something to you with all the feeling I have in my heart. It's the same thing the apostle Paul was saying to the Philippian Christians: Please don't quit! Don't quit on life! Don't quit on your faith! Don't quit on the church! Don't quit on God! Hold fast to what you have obtained; press on.

But the obvious question is, how do we keep our faith alive and well and growing? How do we hold on to our spiritual life? How do we keep from running out of gas spiritually? I have some ideas about that. Let me share them with you.

First of All, Come What May, We Keep On Trusting God Wholeheartedly

This is what the apostle Paul was saying to the Philippians: "I press on toward whatever future lies ahead, trusting God to be there for me." This is wholehearted, unflinching trust in God, and it is so basic and so crucial in the Christian faith.

Shortly before he died, Henri Nouwen wrote a book called *Sabbatical Journeys*. In that book he mentions a family of trapeze artists known as "The Flying Rodleighs." He talks about how their act, their performance, their livelihood, their survival is so dependent on trust in one another. And Nouwen is so right. Just think of it, that special and unique relationship that exists between the flyer and catcher in trapeze acts. The flyer lets go of his swing, saling through the air toward the catcher on the other swing, releasing at just the right moment, and flying in an arc toward the catcher, trusting the catcher to grab him or her. It is an act of total, complete, absolute trust (*Sabbatical Journeys: The Diary of His Final Year,* New York, Crossroad Publishing, 1998).

In the Christian faith, we are the flyer and God is the catcher, which means that we do our best and trust God for the rest. We fly toward God and toward the future and trust God to be there for us, to catch us, and to save us.

Have you heard the story about the man who was marooned on a deserted island, like Tom Hanks in the movie *Cast Away*? This man prayed feverishly for God to rescue him, and every day he scanned the horizon for help, but no luck! No one knew he was there. No one was coming to save him. Exhausted, eventually he managed to build a little hut out of driftwood to protect him from the elements and to store his few possessions.

But then one day, the man went out searching for food. When he returned, he found his little hut in flames. The hut was blazing away, and the smoke was rolling up into the sky. The worst had happened. Everything was lost. He was heartsick and discouraged. "God, how could you do this to me?" he cried.

Early the next day, however, the man was awakened by the sound of a ship that was approaching the island. It had come to rescue him. "How on earth did you find me? How did you know I was here?" the man asked his rescuers. They said, "We saw your smoke signal!"

It is so easy to get discouraged when things are going bad. But we need not lose heart, because God is at work in our lives. Even in the midst of our pain and suffering and disappointment, and even at the place of death, we can trust God to be there for us. We can trust God to catch us. So, we do our best and trust God for the rest.

To keep our faith alive, to keep our faith from running out of gas, come what may, we just keep on trusting God wholeheartedly.

Second, Come What May, We Keep On Performing the Holy Habits Regularly

To keep our faith alive and well and growing, it is so essential that we keep on performing "the holy habits." Praying daily, attending Sunday school and church faithfully, studying the Bible conscientiously—these holy habits are so essential and so vital. These are the things that feed and fuel our souls. The hymn writer put it like this:

> Take time to be holy,
> speak oft with thy Lord;
> abide in him always,
> and feed on his word.
> Make friends of God's children,
> help those who are weak,
> forgetting in nothing
> his blessing to seek.
> ("Take Time to Be Holy," William D. Longstaff, 1882)

A few years ago a man wrote a letter to the editor of a newspaper and bluntly complained that it did him no good to go to church every Sunday. "I've gone for thirty years now," he wrote, "and in that time I have heard something like 3,000 sermons. But for the life of me, I can't remember a single one of them. So I think I'm wasting my time, and the pastors are wasting theirs by giving sermons at all."

Well, as you can imagine, that letter started a real controversy in the "Letters to the Editor" column, much to the delight of the editor. Letters came pouring in day after day. This went on for weeks until a man wrote this clincher:

> I've been married for 30 years now. In that time my wife has cooked some 32,000 meals. But, for the life of me, I cannot recall the entire menu for a single one of those meals. However I do know this: They all nourished me and gave me the strength I needed to do my work. If my wife had not [cooked] these meals, I would be physically dead today. Likewise, if I had not gone to church for nourishment, I would be spiritually dead today.

We are spiritually fed by the holy habits, and habits are exactly what they are. Going to church is a habit, and *not* going to church is a habit. Praying is a habit, and *not* praying is a habit. But you see, praying regularly, studying the scriptures, participating in the life and worship of the church family—these are important habits to cultivate in our lives because they feed us. They make us strong spiritually. They enable us to grow spiritually. They keep us alive spiritually. They fuel us spiritually and keep us from running out of gas. They help us hold fast to what we have attained.

So, to keep our faith alive and well, come what may, we keep on trusting God wholeheartedly, and we keep on performing the holy habits regularly.

Third and Finally, Come What May, We Keep On Loving Other People Sacrificially

Jesus referred to this spirit of sacrificial love as the key sign of discipleship (see John 13:34-35).

Their names are Connie and Scott. They are members of our church, a delightful young couple with two beautiful children. They married in 1988, and a year later, Connie went in to the doctor's office for a checkup. Routine tests revealed that Connie had high blood pressure and excess protein in her body. More tests revealed that she had a degenerative kidney disease in which the kidneys attack themselves. She was told that in four to ten years, her kidneys would fail altogether.

Connie did pretty well for a while, and in 1997 she and Scott became parents to a wonderful son, Tait. By the time Tait was two years old, Connie had to have dialysis constantly. Scott said that watching her suffer was so painful. He would wake up at night and find Connie doubled over in pain in the closet, trying to keep quiet so as not to disturb his sleep.

Finally they both realized that Connie's only hope for survival was to have a kidney transplant. Family members offered to donate their kidneys, but the match was not right for any of them. Frightened and deeply concerned, Connie and Scott told their Sunday school class what they were going through and asked for their prayers. The class members did pray for them, but they also did much, much more.

Can you believe it? Four men from the Sunday school class offered to donate one of their kidneys! After eight hours of testing and giving twenty-five vials of blood, one of those men, a young man named Chris, proved to be a perfect match. So in November 1999, Connie and her friend Chris checked into the hospital for the kidney transplant. They took one of Chris's kidneys and implanted it into Connie's body. Immediately, the kidney began pumping, and it worked beautifully. Connie's husband, Scott, said that as soon as they came out of surgery, "You could see the color in Connie's face and the sparkle in her eyes, and now there is this new person with new life and energy that's just indescribable."

Meanwhile, just down the hall, Chris was recovering quickly. He said, "It's pretty weird walking into the hospital as a healthy fellow and coming out all sore and achy, but I've been taught all my life at home and at church that it is important to love and help other people, so it was an easy decision. I'm glad I could help."

A month later, Chris played a round of golf and shot a 79. A year after the surgery, Connie and Scott became parents again, this time to a beautiful daughter. In gratitude to Chris, they named their daughter after him. Her name is Christina, and today both of Connie and Scott's children love Chris. They call him Uncle Chris.

When I first heard about Chris's gift to Connie, I thought of that wonderful scene in the third chapter of the book of Acts where the man who cannot walk asks Simon Peter and John for money, and Peter says to him, "I have no silver or gold, but what I have I give you; in the name of Jesus Christ of Nazareth, stand up and walk" (verse 6).

In similar fashion, Chris had said, in effect, to Connie, "I have no silver and gold, but what I have I give to you in the name of Jesus Christ; I give you my kidney that you may live." And in that moment, somewhere in heaven God was smiling at this incredible act of sacrificial love.

How do we keep our faith alive? How do we keep from running out of gas spiritually? Well, come what may, we keep on trusting God wholeheartedly, we keep on performing the holy habits regularly, and we keep on loving other people sacrificially.

3. EXCITEMENT IN GOD

"I've Got a Strong Case of the 'Can't Help Its'"

Scripture: John 1:35-42

O ne of the great celebrative anthems that comes to us out of African American culture is the powerful spiritual "Ain't Got Time to Die." It was written by Hall Johnson, and it contains these joyfully dramatic words: "Been so busy serving my Master / Ain't got time to die."

In this inspiring and wonderful spiritual, the composer is underscoring and celebrating the joy and excitement of being a Christian, the joy and excitement of serving our Lord in gratitude for what he has done for us.

The point that this spiritual is trying to drive home to us with great enthusiasm is that when we really become Christians, when we really commit our lives to Christ, then we can't sit still. We become so excited, so thrilled, so grateful for our new life in Christ that we can't help but love him, praise him, serve him, and share him with others.

This is precisely what happened to Andrew. He found the Messiah, he encountered Jesus, and he was so excited that he couldn't sit still. Immediately, gratefully, excitedly, he ran to share the good news with his brother Simon. It reads like this in the first chapter of John's Gospel: "[Andrew] first found his brother Simon and said to him, 'We have found the Messiah'" (John 1:41).

Then Andrew brought Simon Peter to Jesus. This was the greatness of Andrew. He was the man who was always introducing others to Jesus. Three different times in the Bible, Andrew comes to center stage, and each time he is bringing someone to meet Jesus.

In his commentary on John, William Barclay reminds us that here in John 1, Andrew brings his brother Simon Peter. In John 6, Andrew brings to Jesus the boy with the five loaves and two fish. And in John 12, we find Andrew bringing to Jesus the inquiring Greeks who wanted to meet Jesus and visit with him (see William Barclay's quotation on p. 117 of this book).

Andrew's greatest joy was sharing the good news of Christ and bringing others into the presence of Christ. Having found Jesus, he could not sit still, he could not help it; he had to share Christ with others.

A minister friend of mine tells about a woman in his church who is so excited to be a Christian. She had a troubled past and had pretty much hit bottom when a friend reached out to her and brought her to church. The church members welcomed her warmly and loved her into the circle of their love and God's love. The woman started going to church faithfully. She joined a wonderful Sunday school class. She began studying the Bible daily. She started praying regularly. And in the process of this she was converted. She realized for the very first time in her life that God loved her, even her! She came to understand that even though she had done all those sordid things in her earlier life, God still loved her, forgave her, accepted her, valued her, and treasured her. She was absolutely bowled over by that "amazing grace," and she committed herself to Christ, heart and soul. Recently she said to her minister, "I'm so excited to be a Christian, that I've got a strong case of the "can't help its"!

This was also true of Andrew. He too had a strong case of the "can't help its." He was so grateful, so thrilled, so excited about Christ that he just could not sit still. *He could not keep Jesus to himself.*

You know, as I think about this, and as I think about my own personal life and spiritual pilgrimage, I can tell you that I too have a strong case of the "can't help its." It goes with being a Christian. Let me show you what I mean by speaking out of my own personal life with three thoughts. Try these on for size with me. I'm sure that you will think of others out of your own personal and spiritual life, but for now, let me share these three with you.

First of All, Because We Are Christians, We Can't Help But Be Grateful

Andrew, along with the people of his time, was longing for a Messiah to come, hoping for a Messiah, praying for a Messiah. When he found the Messiah in Jesus, he was incredibly grateful. You know, there is no such thing as an ungrateful Christian. Christianity by definition is our grateful response to God for his love of the world and his gift to the world of Jesus Christ. Responsive gratitude. That's what Christianity is all about.

A group of young students were asked by their schoolteacher to make a list of what they thought were the present-day seven wonders of the world. Although there were some disagreements, the following seven things received the most votes:

1. the Great Pyramids of Egypt
2. the Taj Mahal
3. the Grand Canyon
4. the Panama Canal
5. the Empire State Building
6. St. Peter's Basilica
7. China's Great Wall

While gathering the votes, the teacher noted that one quiet student had not turned in her paper yet. So the teacher asked the girl if she was having trouble with her list. The girl replied, "Yes, a little. I couldn't quite make up my mind because there were so many." The teacher said, "Well, tell us what you have. Read your list, and maybe we can help."

Hesitantly, shyly, the girl stood up and then read her paper out loud to the class. She said, "I think the seven wonders of the world are:

1. to be able to see
2. to be able to hear
3. to be able to touch
4. to be able to feel
5. to be able to taste
6. to be able to laugh
7. to be able to love."

The room was so quiet when she finished that you could have heard a pin drop. Isn't it amazing how we overlook and take for granted the gifts that God has given us? We become so captivated by man-made things that we sometimes forget the astounding generosity of God.

The psalmist did not make that mistake. Read the psalms. They resound on page after page with praise and gratitude to God. The One Hundredth Psalm is a classic example:

Make a joyful noise to the LORD, all the earth.
    Worship the LORD with gladness;
    come into his presence with singing.
Know that the LORD is God.
    It is he that made us and we are his;
    we are his people, and the sheep of his pasture.
Enter his gates with thanksgiving,
    and his courts with praise.
    Give thanks to him, bless his name.
For the LORD is good;
    his steadfast love endures forever,
    and his faithfulness to all generations.

This is just a sample of how the psalms reverberate with gratitude. That same theme of praise and gratitude is still very much in evidence in our present-day hymnals. Hymns such as "How Great Thou Art," "Now Thank We All Our God," "Come, Ye Thankful People, Come," "Sing Praise to God Who Reigns Above," "O For a Thousand Tongues to Sing," "Joyful, Joyful We Adore Thee," and hundreds more like these great hymns of gratitude fill our hymnals and our hearts.

Why? Because the great theme of our Christian faith, hope, and love is the spirit of gratitude—gratitude for God's presence with us, for God's watchcare over us, for God's forgiveness of us, for God's salvation for us.

A missionary in Africa was preaching his first sermon in a mission church. When the time came for the offering, the people danced their offerings forward. They danced and sang praise to God as they brought their offerings to the altar. It was a beautiful moment.

After the service, the missionary asked one of the people, "Why do you dance and sing when you bring your offering forward on Sunday morning?" Back came the answer: "How could we not dance? We are so grateful to God for what he has done for us in sending Jesus Christ to save us, that we have to dance and sing our thanksgiving; and besides, it says in the Bible, God loves a cheerful giver."

Let me ask you something. Do you feel gratitude to God that strongly? Do you have a strong case of the "can't help its" when it comes to gratitude? When you are a Christian, gratitude is the spirit of your lifestyle. When you are a Christian, you can't help but be grateful!

Second, Because We Are Christians, We Can't Help but Be Confident

This is why Andrew kept bringing people to Christ—because of his confidence in the Lord. Things were not always perfect, times and situations were sometimes hard, but Andrew never lost his confidence in Christ. He just did his best and then trusted God to bring it out right.

Someone once asked the great Christian Phillips Brooks why he seemed always to be so serene and poised and optimistic and confident. I love Phillips Brooks's answer. He said simply, "I am a Christian."

Bob Perk tells a wonderful story about a father and daughter who were in their last moments together at the airport. The airline had announced her departure, and standing there near the security gate, they hugged, and the father said, "I love you, and I wish you enough." She replied, "Dad, our life together has been more than enough. Your love is all I ever needed. I love you so much, and I wish you enough, too, Dad." They hugged and held each other tightly, and then she turned and left. The father walked over toward the window to watch his daughter's plane take off. Tears rolled down his cheeks.

Another man had been watching them. The father turned to the man and said, "Did you ever say good-bye to someone knowing that you would not see each other again in this lifetime?"

"Yes, I have," the man said. "Please forgive me for asking, but why is this a final good-bye?"

The father answered, "I am old now, not in good health, and the real truth is that her next trip back will be for my funeral."

"I'm sorry," said the stranger.

"It's okay. I have had a wonderful life, and it will soon be over for me. But it's been a great ride. God has blessed me and he has always been with me, and he will be with me in the life to come. I have no regrets. I trust God for whatever is ahead."

The other man said, "May I ask you about something? When you were saying good-bye, I heard you say, 'I wish you enough.' What does that mean?"

The father smiled and said, "That's a wish that has been handed down for many generations in my family. My parents used to say it to everyone. When we say, 'I wish you enough,' we are wanting the other person to have enough good things to sustain them, enough good things to keep them happy and faithful and appreciative and fulfilled and strong and confident.

The father looked at the other man and said, "I wish you enough," and then he turned and walked away.

Because we are Christians, we can be confident because in Christ, God gives us enough—enough strength to keep us going, enough forgiveness to make us a new creation, enough courage to enable us to stand tall when times are tough, enough assurance to convince us that ultimately God wins—and he wants to share his victory with us.

This is the good news. Nothing can separate us from God's love and grace. Nothing—not trouble or pain or heartache or disappointment, not even death—can cut us off from God and his love. God is always with us. That is God's promise. So, because we are Christians, we can be grateful and we can be confident.

Third and Finally, Because We Are Christians, We Can't Help but Be Loving

Again, Andrew is a great example of love. He was bighearted, magnanimous, and generous. He was a loving, caring person who was eager to share and anxious to help others. If only we could learn that lesson from Andrew, life would be better for all of us.

Her name is Donna. Donna is a member of our church. She is a mentor in our Kids Hope USA program. Every week she goes to a nearby elementary school to be a friend, encourager, and mentor to a little boy named John. John is about six or seven years old, and Donna and John have bonded in a beautiful way. Though there is quite a difference in their ages, Miss Donna, as John calls her, has become John's best friend. Once each week, she visits him at school and helps him with his school work, and then "going the second mile" every Saturday, Donna takes John to do exciting things that without Donna, John would likely never get to do, things such as visiting the zoo and going to the museum.

A few months ago, Donna's husband died in his sleep. Little John came to the funeral to support his friend Miss Donna in her grief. At the reception after the memorial service, John stood beside Donna and held her hand. She had been there for him, and now he was there for her. He would not leave her side. It was a beautiful moment, and people in the room had tears in their eyes, so touched by John's intense commitment to lovingly stand by Miss Donna, his friend and mentor.

Some of us saw John eyeing the goodies on the reception table—punch and chocolate chip cookies in abundance—and someone said to him, "John, would you like to walk over here and have some refreshments?" But no, he would not leave Donna's side. "I want to stay here with Miss Donna," he would say. The love between the two of them was so radiant and powerful in that room.

Also in the room that day was a man from Chicago. He had flown all the way from Chicago to Houston to be with Donna. Do you know why? Because thirty-eight years ago, when he was in the first grade, Donna had been his mentor at an elementary school in the Chicago area. This man flies from Chicago to Houston every summer to see Donna and to thank her for what she did for him all those years ago, and he had made this special trip to be with Donna when her husband suddenly had died. That man from Chicago says to Donna every time he comes, "I am what I am today because of the love and support you gave me all those years ago." He says, "Miss Donna, you were the first person in my life who believed in me." And today little John says to her in words and actions, "Miss Donna, I love you. I know you love me. You are my best friend."

Now, where did Donna learn to love like that, to reach out to people in need like that, to make a difference in people's lives like that? You know, don't you? The same place the disciple Andrew learned it: from Jesus. You see, when you are a Christian, you get a strong case of the "can't help its." You can't help but be grateful, you can't help but be confident, and you can't help but be loving.

4. DISCIPLES OF GOD

"Dear Hope, Keep Living Up to Your Name"

Scripture: Galatians 6:14-18

I n her wonderful Mitford Years series of books, Jan Karon has written a book called *Shepherds Abiding*. There are many wonderful lines in that book, but one line in particular spoke to me.

A young woman named Hope is going through a difficult time of transition. She wants to become owner of the bookstore where she works in the little town of Mitford, North Carolina.

The name of the bookstore is Happy Endings. Hope has come up with a bold but risky plan to acquire the bookstore, but she is having trouble getting everything to fall into place at the right time. She is worried, anxious, nervous, frightened, and getting close to discouragement when she receives a letter that has only one sentence. The letter reads: "Dear Hope, keep on living up to your name."

That is *our* calling, isn't it—to live up to our name as Christians.

The name "Christian" means

follower of Christ,
disciple of Christ,
one who is of Christ.

If a Houstonian is a person who lives in Houston, then a Christian is one who lives in Christ—one who is Christlike!

And that's how we live up to our name as Christians. We take what Jesus has taught us in words and deeds, and we try our best to live in that spirit. We pray that through the miracle of his grace and through the presence of the Holy Spirit in our hearts, we may become Christlike in our living.

Some years ago, when our daughter Jodi was born, I was standing at the window of the nursery in the hospital in Jackson, Tennessee, with my nose pressed against the glass, looking at our newborn baby, our daughter, our first child.

In those days, they wouldn't let the new father anywhere near the baby. It's so much better now, but back then the fathers were treated like we had some rare form of leprosy, and the dads were kept far away from the babies. They would only let us look at our babies through the nursery window.

That night as I stared at our new daughter, suddenly it hit me: *I'm a father! I'm a dad! I'm a parent!* And as I thought of the joy and privilege and responsibility of that, my mind drifted back to my parents and all that they had done for me.

I thought of the time I got lost at the circus as a little boy, and how my dad (like an early version of *Finding Nemo*) came and found me and lovingly brought me back into the family circle.

And I thought of the time I had a horrible ear infection, and my mother held me and rocked me all night long.

And I thought of the Sunday afternoon when I had appendicitis and they rushed me to the hospital for emergency surgery, and how in the hospital they never left my side.

And I thought of birthdays and Christmases and Thanksgivings and family reunions and vacations.

And I thought of how my parents had worked hard to feed us children and clothe us and help us get educated.

And I thought of my mother and what she went through when Dad died (my parents were only in their thirties at the time), how she so suddenly had to be the sole supporter for our family (with three young children), and how she was able against all odds to rise to the occasion and hold our family together.

On and on I could go documenting the sacrificial love of my parents. And I thought to myself, *How do you repay that? How do you measure that? How do you express your gratitude for that?*

Words aren't big enough. Gifts are not sufficient. There is not enough money in the world to repay my parents for what they have done for me. So, what do I do? I "pay it forward"! I pass it on! I repay them by becoming a good parent to my children.

On a deeper level, think of this. How do we repay Jesus Christ for what he has done for us? How do we express our thanks to him for his sacrificial and redemptive love for each one of us?

The only way we can: We pay it forward. We pass it on. We dedicate our lives to becoming the best Christians we can be; or in other words, we try our best (with the help of God) to live up to our name "Christians." We try our best with the help of God to become Christlike.

In his letter to the Galatians, the apostle Paul expressed it like this. The Galatians had doubted him, questioned his authority, and in essence he said to them:

Nobody has to wonder who I am.
Nobody has to ask what I stand for.
Nobody needs to question my allegiance to Christ and his church, because I have the marks of Jesus branded on my body.
Clearly, without question, I am a slave for Christ.

The Galatians had doubted Paul. They wondered about this one who had persecuted the Christians so arduously only a short time before. They questioned his theology, his apostleship, his authority.

In answer, Paul said to the Galatians: "Look here! You don't have to wonder about me. Anyone can see that I belong to Christ! Look at my life! I am a Christian, and I am giving it all I've got to live up to that name."

Let me ask you something: Can *you* say that? Can people look at you and see clearly that you are a Christian? Do you bear in your life the marks of Christlikeness? Are you living up to the name "Christian"?

Well, how do we do that? Let me share with you three thoughts about it. I'm sure you will think of others, but for now let's look together at these three.

First of All, as Christians We Live Up to Our Name When We Live with Christlike Commitment

When we study the life of Jesus we strongly notice his commitment to the Father, his unflinching, unwavering, unshakable commitment to do God's will. One of the key themes of Jesus' prayer life was "thy will be done."

We see it in The Lord's Prayer, and we see it again in the Garden of Gethsemane as Jesus prays on the night before he goes to the cross. Jesus was determined and committed to do his Father's will.

Later, the apostle Paul exhibited that kind of Christlike commitment. From the moment he encountered Christ on the Damascus Road, Paul was so bowled over by God's gracious love for him and forgiveness of him that he was intensely determined and committed to serve the Christ who had saved him, and he was a bit offended that the Galatians couldn't see that. Paul strongly said to them, Don't question my commitment to Christ! I bear on my body the marks of Jesus!

When Paul spoke of the marks of Jesus on his body, he was probably referring to the physical scars he had received because of his consecration to Christ. Physical scars from beatings, floggings, shipwrecks, harsh persecution—all prompted by his undying commitment to Jesus Christ.

But also remember that when Paul used the word *body,* he didn't just mean flesh and blood. He meant total personality, all that we are and all that we have and all that we ever will become.

So when Paul said, "I bear on my body the marks of Jesus," he meant that Christ had claimed his heart, his mind, his soul, his strength, his attitudes, his abilities, his whole being, his total personality.

He meant that the spirit of Christ had pervaded every aspect of his life, that in all he was and did, he was a complete and committed servant of Christ.

How about you? Are you that committed? *Are* you? Do you have that kind of Christlike commitment? Do you, really?

Some years ago I went to visit with a friend of mine. He was eighty-four years old at the time and was without question one of the finest Christian gentlemen I have ever known. For some medical reason that I can't explain, he suddenly had lost his sight. I went out to minister to him, and he ministered to me. Once again I was amazed and inspired by his faith. He said, "Jim, don't you worry about me. I'm fine. For over eighty years. I have had the gift of vision. I have been able to see the beauties and wonders of God's creation. I had my sight, and now I have lost it. Blessed be the name of the Lord! I'm not going to let a little ol' challenge like this shake my faith! God is good and God is with me, and it will be a new adventure that God will see me through."

That is total commitment—Christlike commitment.

How is it with you right now? Are you living up to your name "Christian" by living in the spirit of Christlike commitment?

Second, as Christians We Live Up to Our Name When We Live with Christlike Character

Have you heard about the two men who went camping? The second night out, they slid into their sleeping bags late one night. Lying there side by side, one of them said, "When I look up into the sky at night, I see stars and planets and constellations and galaxies and the vastness of space." He paused for a minute, and then he said to his buddy, "When you look up, what do you see?" And the other man said, "I see that somebody has stolen our tent!"

That's the way I feel sometimes today when I look at our world. Somebody has stolen our tent of character.

> I remember when character and ethics and morality were of prime importance in our world.
> I remember when the Ten Commandments were widely taught and accepted and respected in our world as the spiritual laws of the universe.
> I remember when as a boy I got a grade on my report card on my character at school.
> I remember when integrity and honesty and goodness and virtue were highly valued and touted in our world.

But now, it seems that someone is trying to steal all that away from us.

A young teenage girl was sent home from school one day because she was caught cheating on a test. When her mother tried to talk to her about it, the teenager screamed, "Leave me alone! You don't get it! Everything is different now! Your rules don't work anymore!"

What do you think about that?
Was that young girl right? Have the rules changed?
Do our time-honored guidelines suddenly not work
    anymore?
Do our biblical principles suddenly not fit today's world?

Well, let me tell you what I think. I believe with all my heart that certain values always endure, that certain truths are always relevant. I think it was wrong to steal, wrong to cheat, and wrong to hurt other people in biblical times, and that it's wrong to steal, wrong to cheat, and wrong to hurt other people now.

The ethical guidelines of the Bible are not harsh rules laid upon us to restrict and hinder us. On the contrary, they are God's gift to us to show us how life works best.

For example, if we violate the natural law of gravity, we suffer the consequences; and if we violate the spiritual laws of the universe, we suffer the consequences.

The truth is that most of the time we know what is right and what is wrong, but our problem is that we are learning how to excuse and rationalize everything and how to justify whatever we selfishly want to do.

Instead of embracing and teaching moral principles, our world today sadly is saying to us, "It's not wrong if you don't get caught."

Somebody is stealing our tent of character, and there are all kinds of well-known, dramatic examples in our world today of how the loss of character can come back to haunt us.

There's a story told about a minister who moved to Houston. To become familiar with the city, he decided to ride around on a metro bus that passed in front of his new church. He got on the bus, sat down, and realized the bus driver had given him a quarter too much in change. The minister thought, *What should I do? I should give it back, but then it's only a quarter. Why worry about such a small amount? No one will ever know; no one will ever miss it.*

When it came time to get off the bus, the moment of truth had come. The minister did the right thing. He said to the driver, "Pardon me, sir. This quarter should come back to you. You gave me too much change."

"I know," said the driver. "I did it on purpose. I recognized you when you got on the bus. I was in your church last Sunday. I've been thinking about joining your church, and I just wanted to see what you would do if I gave you too much change. I guess it was wrong of me to test you like that, but Reverend, you passed with flying colors. I'll see you Sunday!"

When the preacher stepped off the bus, he was weak in the knees. He bowed his head and prayed, "O God, forgive me. I almost sold you out for a quarter."

How would you rate your character right now? Are you living up to the name "Christian" by living in the spirit of Christlike commitment and Christlike character?

Third and Finally, as Christians We Live Up to Our Name When We Live with Christlike Compassion

Have you heard about the seventeen-year-old boy who got lost in a coal mine in West Virginia? Suddenly his light went out and he was in total darkness. Terrified, he began to cry. He was certain that he was going to die down there. In desperation, he fell on his knees, praying: "O Lord, help me! O God, please help me."

Then, he noticed something. Kneeling there to pray, the young man realized that his right knee was touching something hard. He felt it. It was a railroad track. He realized that if he kept his hand on that track and followed it, it would lead him out! That's what he did. He held on to the track and followed the track, and eventually it brought him out of the dark, out of the depths of the mine to light and safety.

That's a great parable for us. If we will hold on to the track of love and compassion, no matter how dark some moments may be, the love-track will bring us out and lead us to the light.

As cliché-ish as it may sound, it is still profoundly true: *Love is the answer,* and it is, according to Jesus, the key sign of discipleship!

Do you want to live up to the name Christian? Then live in the spirit of Christlike commitment, Christlike character, and Christlike love!

5. CHRISTLIKENESS IN GOD

"Have No Regrets"

Scripture: 1 Thessalonians 5:16-18

I recently ran across a touching story about a young man named Ted and his friendship with an older woman named Rose. Ted was a college student when he first met Rose. It was the first day of school in the new semester. Ted had just settled into his desk near the front of the classroom. The professor introduced himself and challenged the students to get to know someone they didn't already know. Ted stood up to look around when a gentle hand touched his shoulder. He turned around to find a sweet-looking elderly woman beaming up at him with a smile that lit up her entire being. She said, "Hi, handsome! My name is Rose. I'm eighty-seven years old, and I just wondered if I could give you a hug."

Ted smiled at her and said, "Absolutely!" and she gave him a big hug. "Why are you in college at such a young, innocent age?" Ted asked her.

Jokingly, Rose replied, "I'm here to meet a rich man, get married, and have a couple of kids."

"No, seriously," Ted replied. "I really am curious and interested in what has motivated you to take on the challenge of college at this time in your life."

Rose answered, "I always dreamed of having a college education, and now I'm getting one."

After class, Ted and Rose walked to the student union building and shared a chocolate milkshake. They became instant friends. Every day for the next three months, they would leave class together and talk nonstop. Ted was mesmerized listening to this amazing woman as she shared her wisdom and experience with him.

Over the course of the year, Rose became a campus icon, and she easily made friends wherever she went. Everybody on campus knew her, and they loved her. Rose reveled in all the attention she was getting from the students, the faculty, and the administrators. She was living it up and having the time of her life.

At the end of the semester, Rose was invited to speak at the football banquet. The folks there that night will always remember what Rose taught them. Rose was introduced and stepped up to the podium. But as she began to deliver her prepared speech, she dropped her three-by-five cards on the floor. Undaunted, she leaned into the microphone and said, "It's great to be coordinated!" and everybody laughed. Then she said, "I'll never get that speech put back in order, so forget that and let me just tell you what I know."

Everybody laughed again. Rose cleared her throat and said, "Over the years I have noticed something, namely this: We do not stop playing because we are old; rather, we grow old because we stop playing." Then Rose said, "There are four secrets for staying young, being happy and achieving success ... and I'm going to tell you what they are.

"Secret Number One: Remember to laugh and find humor every day.

"Secret Number Two: Remember that you've got to have a dream. When you lose your dream, you die. We have so many people walking around who are dead, and they don't even know it.

"Secret Number Three: Remember that there is a huge difference between growing old and growing up. If you are nineteen years old and lie in bed for one full year and don't do one productive thing, you will still turn twenty years old. If I am eighty-seven years old and stay in bed for a year and never do anything, I will still turn eighty-eight. Anybody can grow older. That doesn't take any talent or ability. The idea is to grow up by always finding the opportunity in change."

Then she said, "Here is Secret Number Four: Remember to have no regrets. The elderly usually don't have regrets for what we did, but rather for things we did not do. The only people who fear death are those with regrets."

She concluded her speech by courageously singing the song "The Rose." Rose challenged her audience to study the lyrics and to live them out in their daily lives. At the year's end, Rose finished the college degree she had begun all those years ago. One week after graduation, Rose died peacefully in her sleep. Over two thousand college students attended her funeral in tribute to this wonderful woman who taught by example that it's never too late to be all you can possibly be.

Now, I don't know about you, but I liked all four of Rose's secrets for living: to laugh, to dream, to grow up (not old), and to have no regrets. These are all great thoughts to live by, but for now I want us to focus on that last one, *to have no regrets.*

In a sense this is what the apostle Paul was saying to the Thessalonian church. Timothy had brought to Paul a report of troubles in the church; arrogance, hatefulness, laziness, apathy, immorality, and fretfulness were paralyzing the church and stifling their growth as Christians. Paul wrote to them to deal with these problems. He encouraged them to live in the spirit of Christ—not to be hateful or lazy or sinful, but rather to rejoice always, to pray constantly, and to give thanks in all circumstances. He was saying to them and to us that if you will live daily in the spirit of Christ, then you will have no regrets.

Now, let me be more specific and bring this closer to home with three suggestions for us to think about.

First of All, Have No Regrets Regarding Your Compassion

Live each day in the Christlike spirit of compassion.

Last week I saw one of the most powerful and moving expressions of compassion I have ever seen, and I saw it, of all places, on ESPN, the cable sports network. The story was about a seventeen-year-old high school boy scoring a touchdown in a high school football game in McDermott, Ohio. "Well, what's so special about that?" you may ask. "That happens every Friday night in the fall on football fields all over the country." Yes, but not like this! This touchdown was different, you see, because it was scored by Jake Porter.

Let me tell you about Jake. Jake Porter is seventeen years old, but he can't read. He can sign his name, but sometimes he gets the letters out of place. Jake has chromosomal fragile X syndrome, a disorder that causes mental retardation. Jake attends Northwest High School in McDermott, Ohio, where he takes Special Education courses, and he is absolutely delightful. He is always happy, always talking, and every morning when he arrives at school, he goes into the principal's office and signs in on the teachers' register like he is a member of the faculty reporting for duty.

After his Special Ed classes, Jake rushes to the Northwest High School athletic facility to practice with whichever team is in season: football, basketball, track. He never plays, but he never misses practice. Jake will tell you that the coach at Northwest, Coach Dave Frantz, is his best friend, and Coach Frantz has, indeed, taken Jake under his wing.

A few days before Northwest was to play Waverly High in a Friday night football game, Coach Frantz called the Waverly coach, Derek Dewitt, and told him about Jake, and how Jake came to every practice, but he couldn't put him in the game for fear that Jake might be seriously hurt. And Coach Frantz said to Coach Dewitt, "At the end of the game, if the outcome is not in doubt, I would like to put Jake in for one play. We will just let the quarterback hand him the ball and Jake will take a knee. He's been practicing that all week, but I was hoping your boys wouldn't hit him because I don't want him to get hurt. He is number 45, and I'll let you know when we send him in." Coach Dewitt agreed. Before the game that next Friday night, he found Jake during the warm-up time, and they met and visited for a few minutes, and Coach Dewitt was captivated by Jake's happy spirit.

With five seconds left in the game, the opposing team, Waverly, was ahead 42-0. Coach Frantz called timeout. He walked across the field and told Coach Dewitt that he was going to put Jake in, and that he would just take a knee and end the game. But Coach Dewitt said, "No, that's not good enough. I want him to score a touchdown. I'll tell my players not to touch him." Coach Frantz said, "No, no. You will lose your shutout. I just want him to get in for this one play." But Coach Dewitt persisted: "All my players know Jake, and we want him to score."

When play resumed, Jake got the ball. He started to kneel as he had practiced all week, but his teammates stopped him and told him to run for a touchdown. Jake started toward the line of scrimmage, got confused, and turned around and started running the wrong way. They got him turned back around. The Waverly defense stepped to the side, opening a big hole, and Jake started running and grinning the whole way—49 yards to the end zone for a touchdown!

When he scored, moms on both sides cried, and dads slapped each other on the back. Players for both teams held their helmets above their heads in triumph and cheered for Jake. Late that night Jake told his mother that he scored the winning touchdown. He said, "Waverly won the first quarter and the second and third quarters, but I think my touchdown won the game for us, because everybody was so happy. They were all cheering and crying."

It was the kind of magical moment that years from now will cause a number of people who weren't even there to say they were. But not everybody was happy. Some said, "If special education kids want to play sports, let them do it in the Special Olympics." And other hard-nosed, supercompetitive types said, "That isn't football" prompting Rick Reilly of *Sports Illustrated* to say in his article entitled "The Play of the Year" these fitting words:

That isn't football.

No, it became bigger than football. Since it happened, people in the two towns just seem to be treating one another better. Kids in the two schools walk around beaming...

Jake is no different, though, talks all the time, only now it's to NBC, ESPN, and ... CBS and Fox ... (November 18, 2002).

Somewhere in heaven that Friday night as Jake ran for his touchdown, God was smiling because he saw some of his children living in that moment the way he wants us all to live daily, in the spirit of compassion.

So the point is clear. God wants us to be compassionate people. Jesus taught us that over and over in words and deeds, that compassion, Christlike compassion, is one of the highest and most dramatic signs of Christian discipleship. So, have no regrets regarding your compassion.

Second, Have No Regrets Regarding Your Humility

Live each day in the Christlike spirit of humility.

Now, of course, we know that there is a good kind of pride. We should be proud of our church and our children and our nation. But that's not what the apostle Paul was concerned about. Paul was concerned about that brand of pride that makes people arrogant and haughty and hypocritical, the kind of pride that is the opposite of humility.

A woman tried for years to persuade her egotistical husband not to be so arrogant, so self-centered, so set on himself, but to no avail. Whatever the setting, he was always boasting about himself and his own accomplishments. He always saw himself as number 1. He always thought he knew more than anyone else. Whatever the subject, he would bring it quickly to himself. It was always *him, him, him.*

One day that man and his wife were walking downtown. The man saw one of those machines that tell your fortune and your weight. He put in a coin. Out came the little card, and he began to read. It said, "You are a born leader. You have superior intelligence, quick wit, and charming manners. You have a magnetic personality. You are highly attractive to the opposite sex." After reading the card, the man proudly handed it to his wife and said, "Take a look at this! Just read this and see how lucky you are to have me as your husband." His wife took the card. She read it, and then she turned it over and looked at the other side. She handed the card back to him and said, "It has your weight wrong, too!"

Now compare that to this. Somewhere I read that for most of his life, Albert Einstein had the portraits of two brilliant scientists on his wall. One was Isaac Newton, and the other was James Clark Maxwell, a noted physicist. However, toward the end of his life, Einstein took those pictures down and replaced them with two others. One was the picture of Albert Schweitzer, and the other Mahatma Gandhi. He said he had come to realize that he needed new role models, not of success, but of humility.

Arrogant pride can be devastating to our souls. It robs us of our sense of humor. It makes us stuffy and stodgy and pretentious and overbearing and hypocritical, and it destroys the spirit of gratitude within us because it dupes us into thinking we deserve all the credit.

So, the point is clear: God wants us to be humble people. Jesus taught us that over and over in words and deeds—that humility, Christlike humility, is a beautiful sign of Christian discipleship. So, have no regrets regarding your humility.

Third and Finally, Have No Regrets Regarding Your Gratitude

Live each day in the spirit of Christlike gratitude.

One of our most beloved hymns of gratitude is the hymn "Now Thank We All Our God." This hymn is sung in tiny hamlets, small villages, county-seat towns, and large metropolitan centers all over the world. It is sung in country churches and in majestic cathedrals. It was written in the 1630s, and over the years it has become so popular that today it often is sung on occasions of national rejoicing in Germany, in England, and in America. Listen to these powerful words:

Now thank we all our God,
with heart and hands and voices,
who wondrous things has done,

in whom this world rejoices;
who from our mothers' arms
has blessed us on our way
with countless gifts of love,
and still is ours today.
("Now Thank We All Our God," Martin Rinkart, trans. Catherine
Winkworth, 1858)

This wonderful hymn resounds with the spirit of faith and victory, confidence, and gratitude, and you would think that the person who wrote these words had enjoyed a peaceful, bountiful life with many blessings. Nothing could be further from the truth. The hymn was written by Martin Rinkart, who was a minister in the little town of Eilenburg, Germany, for thirty-two years (1617–1649). One year into his pastorate, the Thirty Years War broke out, and his town was right in the middle of it. To make matters worse, in 1637 the Great Plague swept across the continent, and it hit Eilenburg. People died at the rate of fifty a day, and the man called upon to conduct almost all of those funerals was Martin Rinkart. Over eight thousand people died, including Martin's wife. Martin Rinkart sometimes conducted forty to fifty funerals a day.

Tough circumstances in which to be thankful; and yet this was the man who wrote "Now thank we all our God with heart and hands and voices." How could he do that? How could he be grateful in that situation? Because he knew that God was with him. Life was hard. Times were tough. But God was with him, and that's all that mattered.

Isn't it fascinating to note that our greatest expressions of thanksgiving came from people who did not have a lot of material things:

Jesus, who had no place to lay his head;
Luther, in hiding for his life;
Francis of Assisi, who was voluntarily poor;
Helen Keller, who was blind and deaf;
Mother Teresa, who lived out her days in a leper colony;

the pilgrims, cold and hungry at Plymouth Rock;
Martin Rinkart, in the midst of war and pestilence.

You see, real gratitude involves more than counting our material blessings. Now, I hope you will count your material blessings, but remember that as Christians, even if we don't have many possessions, we can still be grateful because God is with us and God is for us. God is our friend, and that is the real source of thanksgiving. God gives us the gift of himself; that is the real source of our gratitude.

So the point is clear: Have no regrets regarding your compassion, your humility, or your gratitude.

6. ETERNAL LIFE IN GOD

"What Do We Believe About Eternal Life?"

Scripture: John 14:1-7

T here is a wonderful contemporary hymn called "Hymn of Promise." In many churches, it is becoming something of a tradition to sing this hymn at Easter, as well as at memorial and funeral services. The hymn was written in 1986 by Natalie Sleeth, a respected and prolific writer of Christian music. She wrote this hymn for her husband, the late Dr. Ronnie Sleeth, who was an outstanding professor of preaching at Vanderbilt Divinity School, and later at Iliff School of Theology. In 1986 Ronnie Sleeth learned from his doctors that he had a terminal illness.

From the date of the diagnosis of his illness to his death was just twenty-one days, and Natalie wrote "Hymn of Promise" for him before he died. Look at the last stanza. In it, we find these powerful words:

> In our death, a resurrection; unrevealed until its season, something God alone can see at the last, a victory.

Natalie Sleeth had her own set of health problems. For several years, she had battled a debilitating disease, and this disease ultimately took her life. Before she died, she wrote a beautiful statement for her grandchildren. She told them of how she began to realize that she was growing older and that her body was beginning to wear out. She told her grandchildren that she talked to God about this and asked God to help her. God had heard her and said, "My child, when I made the world and filled it with people, I had a plan. I wanted my people to have life as long as they could, but not forever on this earth because then my world would be too full with no room for anybody. I planned it so that when it was time to leave the earth my people would come and live with me in Heaven where there is no pain, no sadness, nor sickness, nor anything bad."

Natalie told her grandchildren that at this point, she said softly to God, "Is my time to come and live with you getting closer?" And God said, "Yes, but don't be afraid, because I will always be with you, and I will always take care of you." Natalie then said to God, "But, I will miss my family and friends, and they will miss me!" And God said, "Yes, but I will comfort them and turn their tears into joy and they will remember you with happiness and be glad of your life among them."

So, slowly Natalie began her journey to heaven, and day by day she drew nearer and nearer to God. In the distance, she said, she could see light and hear beautiful music and feel happiness she had never known before, and as she moved toward the gates of heaven and into the house of God, she said her last words: "It's good! It's good! It's good!"

This is the good news of our Christian faith, the power of salvation, the promise of eternal life—that nothing, not even death, can separate us from the love of God in Christ Jesus our Lord.

Some months ago, a college student came to see me. He had come home from college because his grandfather was critically ill. He came into my office, sat down, and said, "I guess I've been fortunate. I have never experienced the death of someone close to me, but now my granddad, who has always been my hero, is dying. He doesn't have much time left. The people at the hospital say, 'It's hopeless,' but you and others here at the church have taught us about another kind of hope." Then, as only a college sophomore could say it, he added, "So, Jim, I want to hold your feet to the fire. Tell me why *you* believe in eternal life."

I reached over and picked up a legal pad from my desk and said, "Let's work on this together. Let's see how many reasons to believe in eternal life we can list." Actually, we came up with several, but for now let me just share three of those with you.

There are many. I'm sure you will think of others, but for now let's take a look at these three.

First of All, We Remembered That the Great Christians Were Not Afraid of Death, Because They Believed Strongly in Eternal Life

There is no doubt about this. The great Christians were not afraid of death. They faced it squarely, confidently, courageously. "If life is Christ," they reasoned, "then death will be more of Christ, and it will not be death at all, but entrance into a larger and deeper dimension of life with God." The great Christians all have been very sure of this. History records it over and over again.

On Sunday, April 8, 1945, Dietrich Bonhoeffer was executed by Nazi soldiers. He had been leading a worship service for his fellow prisoners in one of those horrendous World War II death camps. Just as he finished his last prayer, the door flew open and two evil looking men stepped inside. One of them shouted, "Prisoner Bonhoeffer, come with us!" All who were present knew what that meant. Bonhoeffer was to be executed; he was to die. As Bonhoeffer walked out toward the gallows, he said to his fellow prisoners, "This is the end, but for me, the beginning of life."

Ignatius, the Bishop of Antioch in the early church, as he was led to the arena to be thrown to the lions, said, "Grant me no more than to be a sacrifice for God. . . . I would rather die and get to Jesus Christ than reign over the ends of the earth."

Polycarp, the Bishop of Smyrna, was burned at the stake in the middle of the second century because he would not curse Christ and bow down to Caesar. Polycarp said, "Eighty-six years I have served him and he never did me wrong. . . . I will not deny my King now. . . . I am a Christian." Then as he died at the stake, he said a prayer of thanksgiving to God for the privilege of dying for the faith.

Susanna Wesley, mother of nineteen children, including John and Charles Wesley, on her deathbed called her children and their families to her side and said, "As soon as I am released, children, sing a psalm of praise to God."

John Wesley's own famous last words were words of great faith: "The best of all is God is with us."

The apostle Paul, as he faced death, spoke to his Philippian friends with a heart overflowing with joy, and he said, "Rejoice in the Lord always; again I will say, Rejoice.... For to me, living is Christ and dying is gain" (Philippians 4:4, 1:21).

And remember also the powerful words of Henry Van Dyke in his *Parable of Immortality:*

> I am standing on the seashore. A ship at my side spreads her white sails to the morning breeze and starts for the blue ocean. She is an object of beauty and strength, and I stand and watch until at last she hangs like a speck of white cloud just where the sea and sky come down to mingle with each other. Then someone at my side says, "there she goes!"
>
> "Gone where?" Gone from my sight—that is all. She is just as large in mast and hull and span as she was when she left my side and just as able to bear her load of living freight to the place of her destination. Her diminished size is in me, not in her. And just at the moment when someone at my side says, "There she goes!" there are other eyes watching her coming and other voices ready to take up the glad shout, "Here she comes! Here she comes!" on the other shore.

Now, why did these great Christians, and millions and millions of Christians who came along after them, believe so unwaveringly, so unflinchingly, in eternal life? Why were they so unafraid of death? Where did they get such strength and serenity and confidence? You know the answer to that, don't you? They got it from Jesus. And that brings us to point number two. As the college student and I made our list of why we believe in eternal life, first, we remembered that the great Christians were not afraid of death, because they believe in eternal life.

Second, We Remembered What Jesus Taught Us About Life After Death

Jesus not only conquered death through his resurrection; he also taught us that there is life after death for us, and he told us that he would go there and prepare a place for us so that we might be with him. I want you to think with me for a moment about that word, *place.*

Sometimes we use that word in a bad way: "Keep 'em in their place!" But 99 percent of the time, it is a good and wonderful word. Dr. Fred Craddock expresses it like this:

> I am talking about the word "place." Place. The children ran all through this new little house, a bath and five rooms built by volunteers with Habitat for Humanity. That woman and those three little girls stood there, that woman's eyes brimming with tears and the children running into each room and back then pulling at her skirt. "Mama, is this our place? Mama, is this our place?" Off they'd run and back and she'd say "Yes, yes, yes. This is going to be our place." Look at their eyes, really look at their eyes. I'm talking about the word, "place.".... I was coming out of Cartecay Creek after another unsuccessful day of trout fishing. A man and woman drove up and got out of their car. I said, "Going to fish?" He said, "No." They opened the trunk and got out a couple of those little flexi-chairs, folding chairs. I said, "Oh, you going to have a picnic?" He said, "No." Then, they put the chairs out in front of the car and sat there.
>
> Well, I was ready to go but couldn't stand it, of course, so I said, "What're you doing?" He said, "I'm a minister in the United Methodist Church. I'm going to retire in two years. We've lived over forty years in the churches' houses, so I bought an acre here along the creek ... and we're going to have a place of our own." I'm talking about "place." You have to have that word to understand the Bible. (*Craddock Stories,* St. Louis, MO: Chalice Press, 2001, pp. 85-86)

Isn't it beautiful when you think of the word *place* like that? I believe in eternal life because Jesus told us about it, and he also told us that he was going ahead to prepare a special place for us there.

But also, don't miss this. Do you remember when Jesus was on the cross, just shortly before he breathed his last breath, he prayed a beautiful prayer: "Father, into your hands I commend my spirit" (Luke 23:46). Did you know that this probably was not the first time Jesus had prayed this prayer, "Father, into your hands I commend my spirit"? He likely had prayed it hundreds of times as a child, because you see, this was the bedtime prayer taught to little children during biblical times.

It was the first-century version of "Now, I lay me down to sleep, I pray the Lord my soul to keep...."

"Father, I'm about to go to sleep now, so into your hands I commit my spirit."

"I'm going to sleep now, Father. I know you are here to watch over me, and I know you will be near when I wake up."

It was the prayer of total and complete trust. It was the prayer of total and complete confidence. It was the prayer Jesus prayed on the cross just before he died. And it is the prayer you and I can pray daily because we know that we can trust God; because we know that God has the power to turn the agony of Good Friday into the ecstasy of Easter Sunday; because we know that God has the power to take the cross (the emblem of suffering and shame) and turn it into the greatest symbol of victory this world has ever known.

As someone has said, "We know not what the future holds, but we know who holds the future."

The point is clear: Jesus not only told us about eternal life; he not only told us that he would go before us to prepare a place for us there, but also, in the greatest crisis moment of his life, as he endured the pain of the cross and as he died on the cross for our sins, Jesus wrapped his arms confidently around this belief in eternal life, and he prayed: "Father, into Thy hands, I commit my spirit."

And one more thing: Jesus also showed us dramatically and powerfully through his resurrection that there is indeed life after death.

As the young college student and I made our list of why we believe in eternal life, first we remembered how the great Christians were not afraid of death, because they believed in eternal life; and, second, we remembered what Jesus taught us about life after death.

Third and Finally, We Remembered the Bible's Greatest Promise: That God Loves Us, and He Is with Us on Both Sides of the Grave

Whether we live or whether we die, we belong to God, and nothing—not even death—can separate us from him.

For you see, death is not really death at all for the Christian; it's just a door that we label death that we pass through to enter into a new and larger dimension of life with God.

Now, I could quote Jesus here, or the apostle Paul; but for the moment, let me go another route and ask you to consider carefully the words of a great scientist.

Dr. Wernher von Braun once spoke on the subject "Why I Believe in Immortality," and he said this:

> In our modern world, many people seem to feel that science has somehow made the "religious idea" (of immortality) untimely or old fashioned.
>
> But I think science has a real surprise for the skeptics. Science, for instance, tells us that nothing in nature, not even the tiniest particle, can disappear without a trace.
>
> Think about that for a moment. Once you do, your thoughts about life will never be the same.
>
> Science has found that nothing can disappear without a trace. Nature does not know extinction. All it knows is transformation!
>
> Now, if God applies this fundamental principle to the most minute and insignificant parts of His universe, doesn't it made sense to assume that He applies it also to the masterpiece of His creation—the human soul? I think it does. And everything science has taught me—and continues to teach me—strengthens my belief in the continuity of our spiritual existence after death. Nothing disappears without a trace. (in *The Third Book of Words to Live By,"* ed. W. Nichols, New York: Simon & Schuster, 1962, p. 119)

When someone we love dies, or when we face our own death, we need to remember that—remember that God loves us and that God is on both sides of the grave, and that nothing can separate us from him.

God is there, and that's really all we need to know.

Sometimes when people ask, "What is heaven like?" I feel a little like that five-year-old who answered that question by saying, "I don't know; I ain't dead yet."

Now, that answer is not nearly as childish as it seems. It's really a futile exercise in supposition to try to imagine the exact nature of the hereafter. All we need to know is, God is there!

John Baillie once told a story about this that rang true for me. He told about an old country doctor who made his rounds in a horse-drawn carriage. The doctor's dog would go along with him. One day, the doctor went to a home to visit one of his patients, a man critically ill. "How am I, doctor?" the man asked.

The doctor replied, "It doesn't look good." Both men were quiet for a while.

Then the man said, "What's it like to die, doctor?" The old doctor sat there trying to think of some words of comfort to offer the man. Suddenly, the answer came from a scratching at the door.

The doctor said, "Do you hear that? That's my dog. He's never been in this house before. He has no idea of what's on the other side of that door. He only knows one thing. He knows his master is in here. And because of that, he knows that everything is all right.

"Now," said the doctor, "death is like that. We've never been there, and we don't know what's on the other side of the door. But we know our Master is there, and that's all we really need to know, because since he is there, we can be confident that everything is all right."

God loves us. He cares for us. He has conquered death. He has gone before us. He has prepared a place for us, and he is there. And that's all we really need to know.

7. SHARING GOD WITH CHILDREN

"Train Up a Child"

Scripture: Proverbs 22:6

T here's a story making the rounds recently about an eleven-year-old boy who went fishing every chance he got. He especially loved to fish from the dock of his family's cabin, which was located on a beautiful island in the middle of a gorgeous lake in the state of New Hampshire.

On the evening before bass season opened, the boy and his father went fishing together. They were having some good luck, catching sunfish and perch using worms for bait. But then, the eleven-year-old boy decided to tie a small silver lure to his line and practice casting to get himself ready for tomorrow's bass fishing. The boy made his first cast, and almost immediately his fishing pole doubled over. He knew a huge fish was on the other end. His father watched with pride and admiration as the boy skillfully worked the fish alongside the dock. After quite a tug of war, finally the young boy carefully lifted the big exhausted fish from the water. It was not only the largest fish the boy had ever caught, it was the largest fish he had ever seen—but it was a bass.

The boy and his father looked at the amazing catch in the glow of the moonlight. The father lit a match and looked at his watch. It was 10:00 P.M.—two hours before midnight, two hours before bass season opened. The father looked at the huge fish and then at the boy. "You'll have to put it back," he said.

"But, Dad!" cried the boy.

"There will be other fish," said the father.

"Not as big as this one," the boy said. "This is a catch of a lifetime, Dad." The boy looked around the lake. No other fishermen or boats were anywhere around in the moonlight. The boy looked again at his father and knew what he had to do.

Even though no one had seen them, nor could anyone ever know what time he caught the fish, the boy could tell by the clarity of his father's voice that this decision was not negotiable. He quickly freed the huge bass and lowered it back into the water, and he watched as the incredible fish swam away. It swished its powerful body once, twice, and it was gone. The boy suspected that he would never again see such a great fish.

That was thirty-four years ago. Today, the boy is a successful architect in New York City. His family's cabin is still there on the island in the middle of the beautiful New Hampshire lake. This man now takes his own son and daughter fishing from that same dock.

And he was right. Although he caught a lot of fish over the years, he never again caught such a magnificent fish as the one he landed that night long ago when he was eleven years old. But he does see that same fish, again and again, every time he comes up against a question of ethics. Every time he has to make an ethical decision, he thinks about that fish.

For you see, his father taught him well. His father taught him the difference between right and wrong, but he also taught his son that even when you know right from wrong, it is the practice of ethics that is difficult.

Do we do right when no one is looking?

Do we refuse to cut corners to get the design in on time?

Do we refuse to take advantage of people?

Do we refuse to bend the laws?

We do if we were taught to put the fish back when we were young! The decision to do right, and always to stand tall for ethics and morality and goodness, remains fragrant in our memories if, when we were children, we were strongly taught to "put the fish back."

This is the story we want proudly to tell our children and grandchildren. Not about how we had a chance to beat the system and took it, but about how we did the right thing and were for-ever strengthened.

This is precisely what this powerful verse in Proverbs 22 is all about. Remember how it reads: "Train children in the right way, / and when old, they will not stray" (verse 6).

In my experience, I have found this verse to be true and right on target. Of course, we all know that there are some painful, heartbreaking exceptions in which the parents and the church do everything right, and still a person can get in with the wrong crowd and end up far away from what they were taught as chil-dren. That does happen. But most of the time, the vast majority of the time, children grow up and take on the values that they learned at home. Even if some of them as they grow up go through a period of "sowing wild oats," they most often will come back to the values and ethics and morality and faith they were taught early on as children by their parents, their Sunday school, and their church.

One of the greatest privileges and most awesome responsibili-ties we share at home and in church is the crucial ministry of training children so that they may grow up to become a blessing to the world. It is our sacred job to introduce them to Jesus Christ, to tell them the stories of Jesus, to teach them the Christian faith, to model for them the Christian lifestyle, and to welcome them warmly into the church family.

In recent years, psychologists have emphasized how important the early years are. Our personalities, attitudes, values, habits, principles, self-esteem, and even I.Q. are shaped so powerfully by what happens to us in the first few years of life

I once read a poem called "A Child's Appeal" that touched my heart. The poem, written by Mamie Gene Cole, uses the first-person as if a child is speaking to the world. The child is essen-tially saying, "Here I am, world. You have anticipated my arrival, and now I'm here—ready to find my special place. But I need your help. I need your encouragement. I need your teaching. I need your inspiration. I need your guidance. My destiny is in your hands." The poem ends with these powerful words:

"Train me, I beg you, that I may be a blessing to the world."

Just as we begin training our children physically and mentally when they are very young, so also we must begin training them spiritually in their earliest years. There's an old story about a young mother who asked a noted counselor how soon she should begin teaching her child the faith. The counselor asked, "How old is your child?"

The mother answered, "Two."

The counselor said, "Hurry home. You're three years late already."

The counselor was right. It is best to start early. But let me hurry to say that it's never too late. Starting late is better than never starting at all. Proverbs 22:6 puts it like this: "Train children in the right way, and when old, they will not stray."

How do we do that at home and at church? How do we train children in the right way, so that when old, they will not stray? There are many answers to that question. Let me underscore three of them.

First of All, We Can Train Up Children to Have a Strong Sense of Commitment to Christ and His Church

Now, let me say something to parents and grandparents and teachers (and indeed, to all of us) with all the feeling I have in my heart. You can give your children a cashmere sweater, expensive shoes, a ski trip to Colorado, or an expensive automobile if you want to. But let me tell you something: Without question, the best gift you can give them is Jesus Christ! If you want to do something good for your children, if you want to give them the gift that keeps on giving, then introduce them to Jesus Christ!

Get them completely involved in church. Show them how important your faith is to you. Help them discover the power of the Christian faith.

A minister friend of mine tells about a young woman in his church who was expressing her fears one day. She had just gone through a divorce, and she found herself anxious and fearful about the future. "If it were just me," she said, "I'd be okay. Oh, yes, I would hurt and I would feel lonely and I would have to do without some things, but I know I could handle it. But it's my three kids that I'm worried about." And then she said, "So many of their friends have new clothes to wear to school this year, and not just new clothes, but expensive designer clothes. There's no way I can afford things like that now, and when they reach college age, what in the world will I do then? We're just barely making it as it is."

And with that, her voice trailed off and she began to cry.

An older woman came over, put her arms around the younger woman, and tried to comfort her. "I know just how you feel," she said. "I was in your place twenty years ago. My husband left me. I had four little children younger than nine years of age, and I wasn't even making $500 a month. But, let me tell you something: We made it, the five of us, and I'm so proud of who and where my kids are today. I'd put them up against anybody's kids."

And then she looked at the younger woman and said, "I have only one piece of advice to give you. It's the best advice I know. Make sure you and your children go to church and Sunday school every week. That might not seem like much to you right now, but I cannot tell you what a difference it will make in the long run. They will receive something there that many kids don't receive, and it's something they can build their lives on for the rest of their days. Christ and his church—that's the best gift you can give your kids. Don't ever forget that."

That woman was right, wasn't she? We dare not forget that what really pays off is not what we give children on the outside, but what we give them on the inside—how we nurture them within.

The best way to give children what they need within is to give them Christ and his church, and to let them see us supporting the church, being committed to Christ and his church.

Now, of course we can't make that decision for them. It's a personal decision, for sure. But we can strongly encourage them in that direction.

That's number one: It's so important that we train up our children to have a strong sense of trust in, and a commitment to, Christ and his church.

Second, We Can Train Up Children to Have a Strong Sense of Self-Esteem

Recently I read a story about a little girl who was sitting in her grandfather's lap. He was reading her a bedtime story. Every now and then she would take her eyes off the book and reach up and touch his wrinkled cheek. Then in turn, she would touch her own cheek, and then his again. Finally she said, "Granddaddy, did God make you?"

"Yes, sweetheart," he said, "God made me a long time ago."

Then she said, "Granddaddy, did God make me, too?"

"Yes, indeed, honey," he assured her. "God made you just a little while ago."

"Oh," she said. Then feeling their respective faces again, she said, "God's getting better at it, isn't he?"

That little girl has a beautiful and strong sense of self-esteem, doesn't she? And that's a good thing. Let me show you why.

One of the great programs we participate in at our church is called Kids Hope USA. Kids Hope USA was founded some years ago by a minister named Virgil Gulker. His dream was to create a program in which caring adults would become mentors for at-risk children. Each mentor is well trained to love the child, to affirm the child, to encourage the child, to befriend the child, to work with the child to enhance the child's self-esteem. Many of the children have no one in their lives saying, "I care about you and I believe in you!"

The results are amazing. As the child's self-esteem goes up, so do his or her grades. Sociologists tell us that at-risk children basically operate out of the lower part of the brain. All the energy goes there because they are mainly trying to survive. Their over-riding attitude in every situation is "fight or flight": *Do I fight to survive, or do I run away to survive?*

But then when the child feels loved and affirmed and valued, that energy moves higher up in the brain cells; and when that happens, the child can learn, the child can think creatively, the child can love back, the child can enjoy happy, healthy relationships.

One mentor here in Houston went to an elementary school to meet Roxanne, the little girl she would mentor. The mentor asked Roxanne, "What is your name?" The little girl's self-esteem was so low that she could not even look into the mentor's eyes. And Roxanne said, "Why don't you just call me what everybody else calls me?"

"And what do they call you?" the mentor asked.

"Most people call me Idiot."

The mentor said, "Well, I'm going to call you Roxanne. That's such a beautiful name for such a beautiful girl."

And each week, the mentor would shower Roxanne with great names the little girl had never heard before: *awesome, wonderful, special, smart, pretty,* and then the one that really touched the child deep in her soul. "Roxanne," she said, "Will you be my *friend?*"

As a result, Roxanne gradually began to behave with confidence in school and in relationships, and she began to acquire a healthy and strong sense of self-respect and self-esteem. Her grades in school went up dramatically, and her number of friends in school increased amazingly.

It is so important, so essential, so crucial to train up children with a strong sense of commitment to Christ and his church, and with a strong sense of healthy self-esteem.

Third and Finally, We Can Train Up Children to Have a Strong Sense of Love and Respect for Other People

Their names are Pam and Scott, a wonderful young couple who are members of our church. After they married, they wanted so much to have a baby, but no luck. They tried for five and a half years, with many disappointments. Finally, late last summer, they quietly applied to adopt a baby. Pam didn't even tell her mother that they had decided to adopt.

On Friday afternoon, December 12, Pam's mother was visiting

Pam in her home. A little before 4:00 P.M., Pam's mother decided that she had better head home and get ahead of the Friday evening traffic on Highway 59. Just a few minutes after her mother left, Pam's phone rang. It was the adoption agency. They said, "Pam, we have a baby for you and Scott, a little boy. He is three days old, and we would like to bring your new baby to you right now."

This was out of the blue, and Pam was so thrilled, so excited. Quickly she called Scott with the incredible news, and then she thought of her mother driving in the Friday afternoon traffic on Highway 59. Pam called her mother on her cell phone and said, "Mom, I need to tell you something, but first you have to promise me that you won't have a wreck on Highway 59."

Then she told her mother, and Mom handled it great. Pam got the call about her new baby at 4:00 in the afternoon. By 8:30, Pam and Scott had their new three-day-old baby in their home. They named him Tyler, and then they realized something. Pam expressed it to me like this. She said, "Suddenly we had a new baby in our home, and we did not have one baby thing in our house. But," she told me, "by 10:00 that evening, our house looked like a baby store!"

How did that happen? Where did all those baby things come from? They came from Pam and Scott's Sunday school class! Class members heard the news and were so thrilled and happy for Pam and Scott that they came bringing everything you would need to care for a baby. Crib, infant carseat, clothes, blankets, baby bottles, formula, pacifiers; they brought it all. Phone calls, e-mail messages, and faxes had gone out, telling the news to the Sunday school class. The class had risen to the occasion, and here they had come with gifts and hugs and tears of joy and love.

That's what's great about the church, and that is the kind of love and respect for others that we need to teach our children and show our children in the way we model and live out daily the spirit of Christlike love, not just toward those in our church and our Sunday school class, but toward every person we meet. It is so important, so essential, so crucial that we do our best, with God's help, to give children . . .

a strong sense of commitment to Christ and his church,
a strong sense of healthy self-esteem, and
a strong sense of love and respect for others.

Now, let me conclude with something every adult should read, because whether we realize it or not, children are watching us and are doing as we do, and not as we say. It's called "When You Thought I Wasn't Looking." This amazing piece was written by Rita Schilke Korzan, and powerfully she describes the things children learn from us when we think they aren't looking. Things such as how seeing us put the picture they painted on the refrigerator encourages them to paint another one, how seeing us helping others teaches them to be caring and compassionate, how seeing us practicing our faith shows them how important God is, and how they, too, can trust God to be there for them. On and on the poem goes expressing beautifully the things our children learn from us (such as life's great lessons of responsibility, thoughtfulness, worship, stewardship, gratitude, and service) when we think they aren't looking. The piece ends with these poignant words: "Thanks for all the things I saw when you thought I wasn't looking."

8. FINDING GOD IN THE BIBLE

"How to Read and Understand the Bible"

Scripture: 2 Timothy 3:14-17

Some months ago, Jay Leno was doing his "on the street" interviews one night on *The Tonight Show*. He asked some college students a few questions about the Bible.

"Can you name one of the Ten Commandments?" he asked. One student replied, "Freedom of speech?"

Then Jay Leno asked another student, "Can you complete this sentence: 'Let that one who is without sin ...'" Her response was, "Have a good time?"

Jay Leno then turned to a young man who had been smugly rolling his eyes and laughing at the answers given by his friends, and Leno asked him, "Who, according to the Bible, was swallowed by a whale?" The young man smiled with confidence and said, "Oh, I know that one—Pinocchio!"

We laugh and joke about it, but the truth is that our biblical illiteracy is no joke; it is no laughing matter. Actually, we need to be very careful as we read and study the Bible. Let me show you what I mean. Turn to 1 John 4:18 in the New Testament. You will find there this beautiful verse: "There is no fear in love, but perfect love casts out fear."

Now imagine that we want to send a telegram of congratulations to a young woman who has just gotten married. To save money, we tell the operator to simply have the telegram read "1 John 4:18." But suppose the telegraph operator doesn't know very much about the Bible, so she carelessly leaves off the numeral "1." So, when our friend receives the telegram, she turns not to the First Letter of John, chapter 4, verse 18, but rather to The Gospel According to John, chapter 4, verse 18. Turn now to John 4:18, and you will see that instead of reading "There is no fear in love, but perfect love casts out fear," the new bride instead reads, "You have had five husbands, and the one you have now is not your husband"!

The point is clear: When we read the Bible, we need to know what we are doing. As our text puts it, "All scripture is inspired by God and is useful for teaching ... and for training in righteousness" (2 Timothy 3:16). But we have to know how to approach the scriptures.

Broadly speaking, people have approached the Bible over the years in four different ways. Let me capsule these four basic approaches for us and then suggest to you what I think is the best way to read the Bible.

First, Some People Approach the Bible Allegorically or Symbolically

Do you remember the difference between an allegory and a parable? A parable, on the one hand, is a story told to make one central point. An allegory, on the other hand, is a story told in which everything symbolizes something. There is hidden meaning, and you have to figure out what is being symbolized here.

Some people read the Bible symbolically, allegorically. They look at it (especially the book of Revelation) and say, "*That's* Russia, *that's* China, *that's* Washington, and therefore the end of the world will be in the spring of next year." This can be a dangerous way to study the Bible because we can bring our own preconceived notions to it and make the scriptures say what we want them to say.

Let me show you what I mean. Here is an allegory:

"The raccoon had a splinter in his paw until he got to the riverbank and washed it away, and then he danced for joy." As a Christian I could interpret that allegorically like this: I am the raccoon, the splinter in my paw is my sin, the riverbank is the church (or baptism), and the dance for joy is the joyous Christian lifestyle.

But how would the cartoon character Homer Simpson interpret that same allegory? Probably like this: "I am the raccoon, the splinter in my paw is that I need a drink, the riverbank is the local pub," and I won't even mention the dance for joy!

Now, that's the danger of interpreting the Bible symbolically, allegorically. We can make it say what we want it to say. We should study the Bible allegorically only when we are studying an allegory.

Second, Some People Approach the Bible Literally

At least, they *say* they do. Now, I'm going to say something that may sound strange to some of you at first, but I think if you will stay tuned in, you will see what I'm talking about. Namely this: I have never met a real literalist. I have met people who thought they were. The truth is that we are all interpreters. A literalist is one who accepts every single word at face value, and not one of us really does that. We all interpret the meanings behind the words.

Let me show you what I mean. Listen to these words:

I slept like a log.
I'm dead tired.
This is driving me up the wall.
I've got a tiger by the tail.
I'm worn to a frazzle.
That singer knocks me out.

You see, we do not take those words literally. We interpret them. Well, the same thing is true in scripture, as when Jesus says, "Become like little children" or "If your right hand offends you, cut it off" or "How can you take the speck out of your neighbor's eye when you have a log in your own eye?"

Do you remember the story about the preacher who called himself a literalist and further believed that every word of the

Bible was of equal value? Consequently, he stopped preparing his sermons. He just flipped open the Bible one Sunday morning and let his finger fall, and wherever it landed that's what he would preach on. But then when he let his finger fall, it landed on the verse that read, "And Judas went out and hanged himself." No sermon came, so he tried again, and this time it read, "Go and do thou likewise." He tried a third time, and it read, "What thou doest, do quickly!"

There are no strict literalists, really. We are all called upon to interpret and to apply the scriptures to our daily lives.

Third, Some People Approach the Bible Academically

This means reading the Bible with the highest level of academic integrity and raising questions such as:

Who wrote this?
When was it written?
Why was it written?
To whom was it written?
What did the words mean back then?
Where does it appear in the Bible?

In other words, we read it in context. Only when we understand the context can we get to the heart of the message.

Have you heard about the young man in Atlanta who wanted to fly to Memphis? Now, of course, we know the context, that Atlanta is in the Eastern Time Zone and Memphis is in the Central Time Zone. But the young man was not aware of that, so there was a little misunderstanding. He went to the Atlanta airport and asked if they had a flight to Memphis. The ticket agent said, "Yes, it leaves at 9:00." The young man asked, "What time does it get there?" "9:01," answered the agent. "Wait a minute," said the young man. "Let me get this straight. It leaves Atlanta at 9:00 and gets to Memphis at 9:01?" "That's right," said the ticket agent. "Do you want a ticket?" To which the young man replied, "No, but I sure want to see that thing take off!"

You see, we need to understand the context. Studying the Bible in context, academically, is a good way to read the Bible, but the only problem with this approach is that it is incomplete. It's helpful, but alone, it's not enough because God is not subject matter; he is our Living Lord. This brings us to the final approach.

Fourth, Some People Approach the Bible Personally

This means reading the Bible in the first-person, seeing it as a personal letter from God, written to us, and then asking

What is this saying to me?
What is God saying to me through this passage of scripture?
How can this help my life at this particular time?

The fatal error that many people make is that they read the Bible as a spectator rather than as a participant. Only when we become a participant in the drama of redemption does the Bible really come alive for us.

Remember how Karl Barth put it. He said, "The Bible becomes the word of God for us, not when we get hold of it, but when it gets hold of us." I would like to suggest that a combination of these last two approaches, combining the academic with the personal, is the best way to read the Bible, asking what did this mean back then, and then asking what does it mean right now for me.

You see, it's good to ask, "Why did Judas betray?" but then I have to ask, "Why do I? Why do I betray?" It's good to raise the question, "Why did Peter deny?"; but for the Bible to become the word of God for me, I also have to ask, "Why do I deny my Lord?"

When the prophet Amos thunders out to the people of Bethel that they are guilty of wrongdoing, we hear him speaking to us as well. He not only tells us what was wrong in Bethel, he is also telling us what is wrong in Houston or Dallas or Portland or Grovers Corners, or wherever we may be living. This means that when Jesus asks, "Who do you say that I am?" he isn't just asking his disciples long ago, he is asking you and me, right here and now.

When Jesus says, "Come unto me" or "Woe unto you," he is not just talking to people long ago and far away; he is speaking directly and personally to us, right here and right now. When we read something like the story of Zacchaeus, we need to ask the academic questions:

Who was Zacchaeus?
Why was he despised?
What was going on in Jericho then?
Who were these tax collectors?
Why did Jesus go to Zacchaeus?
Why is this story found only in Luke?
What did this mean back then?

But we can't stop there. We also have to ask ourselves, "Now what does this story mean to me?" It's then that we see that *we* are Zacchaeus, *we* are up a tree, *we* need Christ to come into our lives and turn us around like that; and he can do it!

When we read the Bible like that—academically, as a student wanting to learn; and personally, as a child of God wanting to obey—that's when the Bible really becomes the word of God for us. So we come to the Bible in the spirit of the hymn writer as he wrote these words:

Tell me the stories of Jesus I love to hear;
things I would ask him to tell me if he were here:
scenes by the wayside, tales of the sea,
stories of Jesus, tell them to me.
("Tell Me the Stories of Jesus," William H. Parker, 1885)

9. LOYALTY TO GOD AND THE CHURCH

"Hold On to the Church with Both Hands"

Scripture: Romans 12:1-2

Some months ago, the Women's Fund for Health Education and Research held their annual fall luncheon at a hotel in Houston. The women members of the Al and Jule Smith family were honored for their volunteer philanthropic service to our community. Since the Smiths are faithful members of our church, I was invited to give the invocation. It was a wonderful occasion.

Over the years, the Women's Fund luncheon has featured some great guest speakers, such as Norman Cousins, Erma Bombeck, Liz Carpenter, and Florence Henderson.

The speaker this year was Charlotte Ford, the daughter of Henry Ford II. Ms. Ford, while being part of the famous Ford family, has in her own right established herself as an entrepreneur.

She is a best-selling author, a successful businesswoman, a fashion designer, a wife, a mother, a grandmother, and a dedicated volunteer, which prompted her selection as Woman of the Year in 1997 by the National Kidney Foundation.

In her speech that day at the luncheon, Ms. Ford talked about her new book, entitled *21st-Century Etiquette*. I liked the way she defined *etiquette*. Simply put, she said, "Etiquette is respect for and consideration of others."

Ms. Ford went on to talk about some new dimensions of "respect for and consideration of others" produced by the new technology of our time, new dimensions such as cell phones, e-mail, and the Internet, the proper use of which she called "Netiquette."

She told a true story about something that happened to her sister on an Amtrak train ride. Ms. Ford's sister had settled into her seat on the train planning to use the three-and-a-half-hour ride as a good time to catch up on her reading.

However, there was a man seated behind her who talked on his cell phone in a loud, obnoxious voice for three straight hours. The man, caught up in his own self-importance, called everybody he knew, and he repeated to all of them the same story:

"I am on Amtrak heading to New York City. I've made reservations for the Esquire Limousine Service to pick me up and drive me into the city. I have reservations at the Hilton in Manhattan. And I have dinner reservations at 21. I have made reservations for the Diamond Limousine Service to pick me up in the morning to drive me out to the airport. And I have reservations for the 10:42 flight to Los Angeles."

On and on this went, the man calling one person after the other, saying exactly the same thing, telling over and over and over about all these reservations he had made in a loud, irritating, obnoxious tone of voice.

Charlotte Ford said that her sister had tried to be patient, but after three hours of this, it became unbearable, so finally she said to the porter, "I don't want to cause a problem, but if you don't mind, could you please ask the man behind me if he could speak a little more softly? I'm trying to read, but I can't concentrate with that loud, booming voice droning on and on, filling the train car."

The porter spoke to the man with the cell phone, but the man ignored him, dismissing him with a wave of his hand and continuing to talk loudly on his cell phone, telling someone else the same obnoxious message:

"I am on Amtrak heading to New York City. I have made reservations with Esquire Limousine Service . . ." and on and on and on he loudly droned.

This went on for three solid hours. Finally, the man got up and went into the men's restroom. As soon as he left, two men who were sitting across from Charlotte Ford's sister motioned for her to come over. She walked across the aisle of the train car, curious to see what they wanted. They said, "We have been hearing the same thing you have been hearing for the last three hours, and we know everything about that man, so we just thought you would like to know that we used our cell phone to cancel all his reservations! The limousine service, the hotel, the flight to L.A., the dinner reservations—we cancelled them all!"

Now, that's what you call "rising to the occasion!"

What I would like to do in this chapter is to "rise to the occasion" by thinking with you about the proper theological etiquette for attending church.

Remember how Charlotte Ford defined etiquette. She said, "It is respect for and consideration of others."

Of course, when it comes to attending church we come in respect for and consideration of others; but even more we come in reverence for God, with respect for God, with gratitude to God, in obedience to God, with love for God, and we come holding hands with one another as the family of God.

Now, with this in mind, and knowing that when we join the church we stand at the altar and make a promise to God to support the church with our presence, let me outline for us three points of theological etiquette for attending church. There are many ideas we could list here, but for now look with me at these three.

First of All, We Come to Church with a Gracious Spirit

This is so incredibly important. God, in his dealings with us, is so gracious, and he wants us to imitate his gracious ways in our dealings with one another. God wants us to live in that spirit, always anxious to love, quick to forgive, eager to reconcile; always gracious toward everyone, gracious in our actions, gracious with our body language, gracious in our words, gracious with our tone of voice.

It's great to come to church. It is greater to come with a gracious spirit. It's so important.

Let me show you what I mean.

Some years ago, when I was a senior in high school and I had just decided to go into the ministry, I was sitting one day in the school cafeteria. One of my classmates named Ted came over. He was the tight end on our football team. He sat beside me and said, "Hey, Jim, is it true what I heard—that you are going to be a minister?"

When I answered, "Yes," Ted said, "You know, Jim, I've never been to a church service in my life."

"Why not?" I asked him.

"Well," he said, "I had a bad experience with a church when I was in junior high school. My family didn't go to church, and I didn't know anything about it. But I was curious. So, one Saturday afternoon when I was in eighth grade, I went into this church building near my home. I didn't mean any harm. I just wanted to look around. But while I was in there, this man came up behind me. He grabbed me and accused me of trying to steal something. He called me a dirty name, and he ran me out and threatened to call the police."

Ted paused for a moment and then softly he said, "I've never been back to church. I know it's unfair to judge the church by that one experience, but to this day when I think of the church, I think of that man—the look on his face, his harsh attitude, his cruel words—and I shudder."

The following Sunday, I took Ted to church with me. He had a lot of questions, but the thing I will never forget was the smile on his face when my church family reached out to him, loved him into the circle, and welcomed him so graciously.

The point is clear: We can turn people on to the church or we can turn them out of the church by the way we treat them.

Our calling is to be gracious, to imitate the gracious spirit of our Lord. That's number one: We come to church with a gracious spirit.

Second, We Come to Church with a Strong Witness

Remember the chorus from that spiritual that asked, "Who will be a witness for my Lord?" And then the last line gives the confident answer: "I will be a witness for my Lord!"

That's our calling as Christians: to be a strong witness for our Lord by the deeds we do, the words we say, and the life we live. It happened in a Sunday school class in a church I served some years ago. I had dreaded that Sunday morning; I had lost sleep dreading that Sunday morning.

There was going to be a knock-down, drag-out meeting that morning, a showdown between two factions in the class. I knew it was coming. I had been forewarned. They had asked me to come and teach after the squabble in class was settled.

Bob Smith had hurt feelings, and he was coming to take it out on the Sunday school class that morning. He was bringing his supporters with him.

Bob was mad at Dick Johnson, and he was going to unleash his anger at Dick and everybody else that morning. Dick had been chair of the nominating committee, and Bob had been left off of some committee that he had wanted to be on, and he was blaming it all on Dick.

Bob was hurt and angry. He felt left out, and for days he had been seething.

That morning, Bob's anger erupted in Sunday school (of all places), and he verbally attacked Dick, and Dick fought back.

Voices were raised. Fingers were pointed. Fists were clenched. Tension was heavy. Jealousy, envy, resentment, pettiness were filling the room.

Finally, the class president got so flustered by the whole thing that he tried to resolve it by calling for a vote. He said, "Everybody for Bob's side, raise your hand." But then came a voice from the back of the room. "Wait a minute. Wait a minute. Before we vote on anything, I want to say something."

It was Mary Beckett. With tears glistening in her eyes, Mary Beckett stood up and began to speak. Oh my, how she spoke!

"What on earth are we doing? This is so ridiculous. This is so wrong! What is all this talk about sides?" she said. "What is all this talk about Bob's side and Dick's side? We are a church! We don't choose up sides. We are all on the same side. We are all on God's side. We are a family here. God's family! Sides? It breaks my heart to hear us squabble like this. It must break God's heart, too!"

With that, Mary Beckett sat down, and there was not a sound in the room. And in the silence, everybody realized that Mary was right, and people were ashamed of how they had been acting.

Then Bob Smith stood up. Nervously, he cleared his throat and softly he spoke: "I am so sorry," he said, "and I want to apologize to all of you, but especially to Dick. I don't know what got into me. Maybe I was jealous. Maybe I felt left out. But thanks to Mary, I know now that I was wrong, and I'm sorry. I'm really sorry."

Then Bob walked over to Dick Johnson. He extended his hand and said, "Dick, can you ever forgive me?" Dick stood up. He shook Bob's hand, and then smiling through tears, he gave Bob a big bear hug. All the class members stood and cheered; and I just stood there and watched the Holy Spirit work, and quietly I prayed, "Thank you, God, for the strong witness of Mary Beckett today."

First, we come to church with a gracious spirit; and second, we come with a strong witness.

Third and Finally, We Come to Church with a Deep Commitment

Let me ask you something.

How are you doing?
How committed to Christ and his church are you right now?
How faithful are you really in supporting the church with
     your presence?

Let me put that in perspective by asking you to think about it like this:

If your car would start one out of three times, would you
     consider it faithful?
If your television only worked 60 percent of the time, would
     you consider it faithful?

If your newspaper delivery person should skip your house every other day and an occasional Friday, would you call that faithful?

If your water heater should greet you with cold water three mornings a week, would it be faithful?

If you should fail to come to work ten or twelve days each month, would your employer consider you faithful?

If you should miss a couple of house payments in a year, would your mortgage holder say, "Oh well, ten out of twelve months—that's not too bad"?

If you attend church once or twice a month—25 to 50 percent of the time—would you say that you're faithful?

Now, that's something to think about, isn't it? We are called to be faithful in attending church, and we are called to come to church with a gracious spirit, with a strong witness, and with a deep commitment to God.

10. NEW LIFE IN GOD

"What Do You Want Me to Do Now?"

Scripture: 2 Corinthians 5:17-21; Acts 9:1-9

Have you heard the old story about a duke and duchess who went for a stroll one morning? As they walked hand in hand through their lavish country estate in Europe, they noticed a man dressed in a stately uniform standing alone in their beautiful back garden. "Who is that man?" asked the duchess. "He always stands there, but I don't know who he is."

"Neither do I," answered the duke, "but I, too, have seen him there many times. He always stands right there."

The duchess decided to investigate this further. She walked over to the man and said, "Please tell me, who are you? Do you work here? Are you part of our staff?" "Oh yes, My Lady," said the man, "I have been your faithful servant for almost thirty years."

"Thirty years? Oh my! And what is your specific job?" asked the duchess.

"I was hired to take care of your dog," the man replied.

"But wait a minute," said the duchess. "My dog died twenty-seven years ago!"

To which the man replied, "Yes, My Lady, that is correct. And what, My Lady, would you like me to do now?"

Strange as it may seem, that old story, with its punchline question, "What would you like me to do now?" actually reminds me of some of the most powerful moments in the Bible. When people in the Bible are dramatically confronted by God, when people come dramatically into the presence of God in the scriptures, two questions always seem to emerge. First, the people say, "Who are you, Lord?" and then fast on the heels of that, they ask,

"Lord, what do you want me to do? What would you like me to do now?"

Think of it: Here is Moses in the wilderness of Midian. He is watching over his sheep. Like the duchess's dogkeeper, he has a comfortable life. He has gone to work for a well-to-do man named Jethro, and he has married the boss's daughter. It's a good life. It's easy, safe, cozy, pleasant, nonthreatening.

But Moses is brooding. He is worried about the terrible plight of his people. Their life is not cozy. They are slaves in Egypt. Suddenly God appears to Moses in a burning bush. Moses takes off his shoes, for he knows this is a sacred moment. He is standing in the presence of God. He is standing on holy ground. As Moses enters into conversation with God, in essence he ends up asking these two questions: "Who are you, Lord?" and "Lord, what do you want me to do now?" We know the rest of the story. God sends Moses to set his people free.

And then, in Acts 9, here is Saul, moving down the Damascus Road looking for Christians to persecute and kill. Saul, too, has a comfortable life. He is well educated and highly respected. He is a religious leader, a Pharisee; and he is about the business of stamping out this new religious group who called themselves Christians. They were becoming a nuisance, so Saul became a bounty hunter, a self-appointed vigilante trying single-handedly to eliminate the followers of Jesus. But then suddenly, the risen Lord appeared to Saul on the Damascus Road. The light of the Lord's appearance was so dazzling that Saul was momentarily blinded. Saul was "bowled over" by the powerful presence of the Lord, and all he could think of at that moment was that he needed to ask these two questions: *Who are you, Lord?* and *Lord, what do you want me to do now?*

We know the rest of the story. Saul was converted and given a new name—Paul—and it was so dramatic, he said that he was a new creature, and he became the great missionary to the Gentile world.

The point is clear: When we come into the presence of God, when we understand clearly who God is, the next question to be asked is simply this: *What do you want me to do; Lord, what would you like me to do now?*

There are many good answers to that question, because there are many things God wants us to do. Let me list some ideas about that, and I'm sure you will think of others.

First of All, Celebrate the Gift of Jesus Christ

God wants us to receive and celebrate the gift of Jesus Christ. That's what happened to Paul that day on the Damascus Road. Jesus Christ came powerfully into the life and heart and soul of Paul; so much so, that from that moment forward everything he did was centered in Christ.

Frederick Buechner, in his colorful way, described Paul's conversion experience on the Damascus Road. When Paul realized he was face to face with the risen Lord, the one he had been persecuting, "Paul waited for the axe to fall. Only it wasn't an axe that fell. 'Those boys in Damascus,' Jesus said, 'Don't fight them, join them. I want you on my side.' And Paul never in his life forgot the sheer lunatic joy and astonishment of that moment.... He was never the same again, and neither in a way was the world. Everything he ever said or wrote or did from that day forward was an attempt to bowl over the human race as he'd been bowled over himself.

"And *grace* was the key word and *Christ* was the other key word, of course. He never forgot how he'd called him by name twice, to make sure it got through, and he wrote, 'I have been crucified with Christ ... it is no longer I who live but Christ who lives in me'" (*Peculiar Treasures,* San Francisco: HarperSanFrancisco, 1993, pp. 129-31).

A chief of police in a major city recently wrote a devotional that has haunted me since the moment I read it. He described how effective a bulletproof vest is, if you wear it. He gave two graphic cases in point.

In the first, he described how early one morning one of his motorcycle officers stopped a red pickup truck that had sped through a stop sign. The police officer didn't realize it, but the driver of the pickup had just robbed an all-night grocery store and was at that moment making his getaway. The driver didn't realize he had run a stop sign. He thought, *The cops know [about the robbery] already,* and in a panic, he pulled out the gun he had used in the robbery and fired. The policeman was hit in the chest at point-blank range and knocked to the ground, seven feet away.

All was quiet for a moment. Then slowly but surely, the policeman stood to his feet. The robber couldn't believe his eyes. *This guy must be Clark Kent!* he thought, and then the robber screamed, "Don't shoot! I surrender! I give up!" The police chief, in telling the story, said, "The officer's life had been spared because he was wearing a bullet-proof vest."

Then the chief went on to his next case in point. He told of how just a few weeks later, another young police officer was shot during a drug raid. The bullet hit this officer almost exactly where the motorcycle officer had been hit only weeks before, squarely in the center of the chest. But there was one major difference: It was a hot summer day, and this police officer had taken off his bulletproof vest! The officer died, and he left behind a wife, three small children, and a bulletproof vest that was in the trunk of his car, parked just thirty feet from where he fell.

Then the police chief said this: "Every police officer believes in bulletproof vests. They work! I doubt you could find a policeman anywhere who doesn't believe those vests save lives. But that is not enough. An officer must do more than believe in vests. He must take his belief to the point of personal commitment. He must be willing to wear the vest and wear it at all times. Even when it is hot. Even when it is uncomfortable."

The police chief concluded his devotional with these words: "And in a similar way, it is not enough to believe that a man named Jesus lived 2,000 years ago. We must take that belief to a point of commitment. We must be willing to take that belief to the point of 'putting on' the risen Christ ... receiving Him as Savior and Lord" (*Illustration Digest,* January 1995, pp. 1 and 2; AA Publishing, P.O. Box 170, Winslow Arizona).

If we were to ask ourselves that question, "Lord, what do you want me to do now?" I think one answer God would give us is this: "Celebrate the gift of Jesus Christ."

Second, Celebrate the Gift of New Vision

On the Damascus Road that day, Paul was blinded for a while, but in a sense, he had been blind long before that day. Later, when his sight was restored, he was given the gift of new vision, a new way of seeing things, a new perspective, a new way of looking at life, a new way of looking at other people, and most important, a new way of looking at God.

His name is John. He is now a successful doctor. John tells a remarkable story out of his own experience. Some years ago, just after his medical training, just as he was beginning his medical career, John developed a serious heart problem. He became a likely candidate for a fatal heart attack. His close friends began to pray for him, but the harsh prospect of a massive heart attack was hard for John to handle; and in his grieving, he began to feel sorry for himself. He became somewhat angry with God: *How could God let this happen to me? How? At the beginning of my career? I worked so hard, prepared so well to be a good doctor, and now this. It isn't fair.*

One morning as John was brooding in his office, his father (a retired doctor) suddenly rushed in. Excited, his father said, "John, get on that phone right now and call the hospital. Tell them we are on our way! Tell them to get ready to operate on us immediately!"

"Operate on us?" John said. "Dad, what on earth are you talking about? You've lost me! What do you mean, 'operate on us'?" His father said, "John, my career is over, and yours is just beginning. I have such great hopes and dreams for you. I've been studying about transplants, and I want us to go to the hospital together today, because *I want to give you my good heart!*"

Let me ask you something: Do you love anybody that much? So much that you would give them your heart? John hugged his dad tightly. Together they cried. That special moment touched John so powerfully that for the first time, his hope was restored. Over the years, John's father had expressed his love for him in so many, many ways, but never more dramatically than in that moment.

The story has a happy ending. John was able to have bypass surgery a short time later, and he was healed. He didn't have to have a transplant. John is now a very effective and beloved physician, and his father stops by the office two days a week to assist him. Through his father's incredible love, John was given a new vision, a new life, a new hope, and was understanding of what God is like. Today he says, "That day when my dad offered to give me his heart, I thought, *Just think, if my earthly father's love is that strong, imagine how powerful is the love of our heavenly Father who gave his only Son for us.*"

What does God want us to do now? Well, he wants us first to celebrate the gift of Jesus Christ; and second to celebrate the gift of new vision.

Third and Finally, Celebrate the Gift of Christian Friendship

When we read the letters of Paul, it's obvious how important his Christian friends were to him. That's one of the greatest things about the church, the great friends we find there. God befriends us and binds us together. He gives us this great gift of Christian friendship.

Tom Pace is one of those unforgettable characters. He was a member of our church staff some years ago. He is now the pastor of a church himself. A few years ago, Tom wrote a beautiful article about his friendship with Kent Kilbourne:

> I first met Kent when we worked on staff together at St. Luke's United Methodist Church in Houston. I was the Minister to Youth, he the Minister to Single Adults. He played the guitar. I played the guitar. He played much better than did I so I never liked to play in his company. But I liked to listen to him play. Kent is one of those people who comes into a room like an eighteen-wheel tandem truck. He pushes a current of air in front of him and stirs up lots of wind behind him.

There is an immense amount of energy in his gait, his countenance, his voice. And those in the room are often caught up in the windstorm and find themselves swept into his energy without even knowing it.

His office was right next to mine, so we spent entirely too much time doing things perhaps unrelated to ministry in either of our fields. We laughed a whole lot together. I remember testing a youth game in the hallway of the church offices, one in which we both had pantyhose on our heads, with tennis balls in each stocking foot, swinging them around-around trying to hit the other without being blasted by our opponent's tennis balls. It happened about the time the Senior Minister and a delegation of bishops came walking by in the hall. Oh well.

We dreamed some together, too. "Wouldn't it be neat if we could be co-pastors of a church together? Boy, would we make that place hum!"

We grieved and worried some together as well. We shared concerns about marriage and family and career and call to ministry and money and ... the whole gamut.

As we grew to know each other better, we became aware and then accepting of one another's strengths and shortcomings. He was too free-spirited and creative and procrastinating ... and I ... well, I was, too.

I write all this in the past tense not because Kent has died, but because Kent and I don't talk so much now. For all I know ... he has become solid and stodgy and dependable and boring. But I kind of doubt it. And while I don't mourn much about his absence, I do miss him. I feel lucky to have such a friend.

Sam Keen writes:

"Friendship ... *Philia* ... the love, the affection that exists only between equals, is at once the most modest and rugged of the modes of love. It is as quiet as an afternoon conversation, but strong enough to survive the acids of time. And while it draws us into our emotional depths, it demands no romantic feelings, no howling at the moon, no explosions of contradictory feelings, no jealousy. It is based on the simplest of the heart's syllogisms: I like you, you like me; therefore we are friends ... and we knew intuitively that without a friend ... the best of lives would be too lonely to bear."

Find some friends and value them. I think I'll call Kent today. (*Bay Harbour UMC Newsletter,* Sept. 19, 1994; Vol. 4, No. 34)

Christian friendship is a beautiful thing to see and experience. It happens when people are drawn together and held together by their love for Jesus Christ and his church. The Bible has a special name for this: *koinonia,* the redemptive fellowship.

What does God want us to do now? Many things, I'm sure, but I'm also sure that among these are

to celebrate his gift of Jesus Christ,
to celebrate his gift of new vision, and
to celebrate his gift of Christian friendship.

11. COMMITMENT TO GOD

"Be Careful What You Lean Your Weight On"

Scripture: Joshua 24:14-15

Some years ago, June and I left our hometown of Memphis, Tennessee, and went up north to Ohio to live for three years. We were in our early twenties at the time, and we had been married for a year when we went up there so that I could go to seminary. While I did my three years of theological school, June finished up her remaining three years of college. To say we were busy would put it mildly.

We both were going to school full time and holding down four jobs between us to pay for school and put bread on the table. I was going to seminary, serving two churches, and working as a janitor on the seminary campus. June was going to college and working as the assistant librarian at the seminary, and as the assistant librarian at the Ohio State Observatory, which was next door to the seminary campus.

During our second year in Ohio, Christmas fell on a Sunday, so we had to devise a Christmas plan. Here's what we came up with:

- Finish all academic requirements, classes, projects, papers, and final exams by Friday, December 23.
- Do our Christmas shopping on Saturday, Christmas Eve.
- Have Christmas Eve Communion at both of our churches on Saturday evening.
- I would preach Christmas morning, and then we would get into our little Volkswagen Beetle with our Christmas purchases from the day before and drive fourteen hours to Tennessee to celebrate Christmas with our families.

This meant that we had to do all of our Christmas shopping in one day. So early on that Christmas Eve Saturday morning, we went to a large department store in downtown Columbus, Ohio. When the doors opened at 10:00 A.M., we rushed into the store that covered four city blocks, and we "covered" every inch of it that day. We didn't have much money, so we had to shop carefully. Finally, late that afternoon, we were exhausted, and I thought we were finished with our shopping. But no, June thought of some more gifts we needed to give, and she decided she would make the gifts in the car the next day on the long drive home.

So we went to the fabric department. Now, I can hang in there pretty well with the shopping when you are just buying ready-made gifts. But fabric shopping is not my cup of tea. I just go weak, all the strength in all of my muscles just goes away, and my legs and arms begin to feel like wet spaghetti. So as June continued to shop for the fabrics she needed, I took the two completely filled shopping bags and started looking for a place to sit down. No luck! There was not an empty chair anywhere in sight. But there were all of these large bolts of material on display throughout the fabric department. All these bolts of material with the fabrics draped this way and that to display them beautifully.

I began to look for a bolt of material I could lean against. Then I saw it—a large bolt of black material over in the corner. It was a perfect resting place, the next best thing to a chair. There I was with those two heavy shopping bags (one in each arm), with instructions from my wife not to put them down. So I went over to the corner and leaned back against that soft bolt of black material.

Oh, it was so wonderful! I was so tired, and it felt so good to lean my weight on that bolt of material. I was resting there so nicely, when all of a sudden I felt this strange sensation. I thought, *I'm so tired I'm just imagining things, but it felt like that bolt of material moved.* And then I realized it *did* move! I turned around. That bolt of black material turned around, and I found myself looking into the sweet, angelic face of an elderly Roman Catholic nun!

I was so embarrassed. My face turned red as a beet, and I stammered out the only thing I could think of to say in that moment. I said, "I'm sorry. I thought you were a bolt of material!" Oh, no. What a terrible thing to say! I couldn't believe I had said that. I tried to say some other things, all of which were wrong, and finally I just blurted out, "I am so sorry!" The elderly nun smiled, she reached over and patted my cheek, and she said, "My son, your sins are forgiven." Then she winked at me and turned and walke away.

Now, the moral of that story can be summed up in a ʰ "Those who look before they lean need not worry nun!"

But more seriously, that story raises a much-needed w for us: Be careful what you lean your weight on! Be where you put your trust! This warning is so fitting for because everywhere we go, there is an incessant clamoring our trust, our allegiance, our energy, our resources, our commitment, the weight of our influence. Everywhere we go, every step we take these days, someone is screaming in our ears loudly or whispering in our ears temptingly: Lean your weight on me. Trust me. Follow me. I am the answer for you. Put your faith in me—money, power, pleasure, self-centeredness, political clout, possessions, fads. They all say to us: Lean your whole weight on me. Give your best to me. Give your energy, your resources and your commitment to me.

Now, this is precisely what the scripture passage in Joshua 24 is all about. Remember how forcefully Joshua said it: "'Choose this day whom you will serve . . . but as for me and my household, we will serve the LORD'" (verse 15).

We will put our trust in God! This is without question one of the greatest statements in all of the Bible. But what was the context of this strong statement? What prompted Joshua to say that?

If you listen to those words closely, you can hear a lot of strong commitment in them, but also a tone of exasperation. You see, after all those years of wandering in the wilderness, the Hebrews had now come into the promised land. They had dreamed of this. They had longed for this. They had prayed for this. But now they were in the land, and now they had a new big problem, and that was the fact that other people lived in this land too. And these other people had their own set of gods that they worshiped: they had a god of war, a god of wine, a god of fertility, and a god of this and that and the other. And some of these false gods looked attractive to the Hebrews. So much so that they actually began worshiping them instead of worshiping the Lord (which, of course, was a blatant violation of the First Commandment).

Joshua saw what his people were doing, and boldly, dramatically, strongly, he laid it on the line. He said, "Choose this day whom you will serve, whether the gods your ancestors served in the region beyond the River or the gods of the Amorites in whose land you are living; but as for me and my household, we will serve the LORD."

This story in Joshua is about choices, decisions, commitments, and priorities. It's about deciding to whom we will give our allegiance, our loyalty, our trust. It's about choosing what we will lean our weight on. Now, let me say three things about that, three strong recommendations.

First of All, Lean Your Weight on Your Family

Joshua said, "As for me and my household …" Family was obviously a priority for him. It should be for us. To underscore how important this is, remember that two of the Ten Commandments call for loyalty to the family. Commandment number five tells us to honor our parents. Commandment number seven tells us to be faithful in marriage. And both commandments remind us that strong families produce a strong nation, and weak families produce a weak nation.

Oh, how we in this modern world need to hear afresh these commandments! Family life is breaking down all around us, and it is tearing our society apart. Drug problems, homelessness, sexual promiscuity, violence, abuse, public profanity, emotional illness, crime; these horrendous social problems are strangling the very life out of our world, and most of them are caused by the breakdown of family life in our time. Nine out of ten people being held in jail or prison today will tell you that their problems are rooted in a bad situation at home, a destructive, often abusive, family life.

Put that over against this: On May 8, 2001, at midday, our church and our city took a blow to the heart. One of our best, Randy Smith, had a massive heart attack and died. Randy, so full of life, so full of faith, so full of joy—so suddenly gone. I'm still having trouble believing it. The next morning, I sat down with Randy's family, with Ann, his wife of over fifty years, and the children, Randy Jr., Meg, and David, to reminisce about Randy. We cried together and laughed together and prayed together as we remembered "Randy stories." At one point I said to the children, "When you think of your dad, what jumps immediately into your mind." Here's what they said:

He always saw the good;
his joy of life;
his sense of humor;
his commitment to Christ;
his love of the Bible;
his love for the church;
his service in the community;
his love for our mom;
his unconditional love for us.

Then Randy's children expressed what I would call three quotable quotes. They said, "His love for us children was the perfect example of God's love." They said, "He treated a federal judge and the parking-lot attendant exactly the same." And they said, "He was the perfect example of what a Christian should be."

Now, think of that. Wouldn't that be something, to come to the end of your days on this earth and have your family remember you like that? It doesn't get any better than that. I was so touched by that experience because it reminded me again that home is where we receive our first instructions in the virtues, our first lessons in right and wrong, our first brush with unconditional love, our first call to faithfulness. The point is clear: Strong families build a strong and virtuous nation. And that's what we need to lean our weight on, not on the latest passing fad, but on the enduring values of the Christian family.

Second, Lean Your Weight on the Church

Now, I deliberately put these thoughts in this order (the church right beside the family) for this reason: We all know that some children and young people and indeed, some adults, are not getting what they need at home. It's sad but true. If that's the case for any one of you, then come to the church. Turn to the church. Let us be your family. Let us give you the love and the discipline and the supervision you need.

I know a young man who had a tough situation at home. His father had deserted the family. They have not heard from the father for years. This young man's mother was doing the best she could. To make ends meet, she had to work two minimum-wage jobs, one during the day and one at night, and consequently she was never home.

So that young man adopted the church as his family, and we adopted him. We became his family. He just pretty much lived at the church. He chose to lean his weight on the church, and now he is one of the finest young men I know. As Ken Medema put it in his song about the church:

> If this is not a place where my tears are understood, where do I go to cry?
> If this is not a place where my spirits can take wing, where do I go to fly?

Be careful where you put your trust. Be careful where you put your hope and confidence. Be careful what you lean your weight on. Lean your weight on your family and on your church.

Third and Finally, Lean Your Weight on God

That's what faith is—it's trusting God, come what may. It's committing your life to God and leaning your weight on him in every circumstance.

Have you heard the story about the little girl who somehow had received a bad cut in the soft flesh of her eyelid? The doctor knew that some stitches were needed, but he also knew that because of the location of the cut, he should not use an anesthetic. He talked with the little girl and told her what he must do, and he asked her if she thought she could stand the touch of the needle without jumping. She thought for a moment and then said simply, "I think I can, if Daddy will hold me while you do it." So the father took his little girl in his lap, steadied her head against his shoulder and held her tightly in his arms. The surgeon then quickly did his work and sewed up the cut in the little girl's eyelid, and she did not flinch. She just held on tightly to her father.

That's a parable for us in our spiritual lives, and a graphic reminder that whatever we have to face, we can hold on tight to our Father, we can trust him and count on him and lean on him. We can lean our whole weight on his everlasting arms.

12. THE SONG OF GOD

"God Gave the Song"

Scripture: Acts 3:1-10

The "good news" of the Christian faith is so great that it's simply not enough to just talk about it. We have to sing it!

There is no way to express in spoken words the deep emotion that wells up within us. We have to sing it! Nowhere is this truer than at Eastertime. The incredible message of Easter, of resurrection, of new life, of Christ's victory over death demands to be sung, cries out to be sung. All the way from a majestic chancel choir triumphantly singing the *Hallelujah* chorus—"For He shall live forever and ever, Hallelujah"—to a little congregation of thirty voices in a small church way out in the country singing at the top of their lungs, "He lives! He lives! Christ Jesus lives today," we sing it, this song of resurrection and life.

In recent years, a new anthem has come onto the scene, one that proclaims the Easter message in a touching and creative way. Youth choirs especially like to sing this anthem. It's called "God Gave the Song." It identifies the song God has given to us as being Jesus Christ and the truth he came to bring. He is the song. His message is the song. His victory is the song.

The anthem begins by telling us that God gave the song, how it came into the world through a manger and how from the beginning some tried to ignore the song or change it or disrupt it or distort it. And finally some were so threatened by the song that they tried to destroy it. They nailed the song to a cross, then they rubbed their hands together and they congratulated themselves on what they had done. At this point, the anthem has these poignant words: "And then they said to themselves: there, that takes care of that ... but it didn't!"

Quietly, but dramatically, the song starts up again because God gave the song; it is always with us.

Now, the most powerful and moving moment in that anthem is where the song resurrects. Some of the people think they have killed it, but it comes back: "What's that I hear? I still hear that music. Day after day, the song goes on." What does that mean? Do you know what that means? It means that the truth of God, the power of God, and the love of God are alive and well in this world. The song cannot be silenced. It cannot be drowned out. It cannot be killed. The song goes on! This means that the possibility of new life is still available to us through the power of the risen Christ. In other words, we too can be resurrected, and we too can take up the song.

There is a fascinating example of this in Acts 3:1-10. It's a miracle story about a man who gets a new chance at life, but it starts out in a very matter-of-fact way.

One day at three in the afternoon, the hour of prayer, Simon Peter and John were on their way up to the Temple. The entrance to the Temple was known as the Beautiful Gate. There was only one thing that marred its beauty: It was a gathering place for beggars. They crowded all around on the Temple steps; and as worshipers came and went from the Temple, they had to thread their way through this mass.

On this occasion in Acts 3 as Peter and John approached the Beautiful Gate, they were confronted by one of these beggars. He had been unable to walk from the time of his birth. He had no way to work, no means of support. He lived literally on charity. As the two disciples started up the steps, the man stretched out his hand in that universal gesture that pleads for help.

Peter said to him, in effect, "Look at us, we don't have any money. We don't have gold, and we don't have silver. We don't even have a trust fund that can be tapped, or a voucher that we can give you, no bus tokens or meal tickets." What a letdown that must have been for this poor man. But then Peter said, "But, we will give you what we have. In the name of Jesus Christ of Nazareth, stand up and walk." Then, notice this. The scriptures say that Simon Peter took the man by the right hand and raised him up! "Raised him up." That means he got resurrected.

It was unbelievable. The man discovered that he could stand by himself, and suddenly he began to dance and skip right there on the church steps. The song was going on, and he was dancing to the beat! People came running from all directions. They knew who this man was. He had been a fixture there for some time. He had been sitting there begging every day for years. Someone always carried him to the Beautiful Gate in the morning, and someone carried him home each night. And now he was jumping up and down like a man possessed.

Peter then said to the crowd that this miracle was done through the power of the risen Christ. It was faith that made it happen. As the story ends, Peter and John and the raised man all link arms and go into the Temple together. Don't you know that at that moment, somewhere in heaven Jesus was smiling, so glad to see his disciples take up the song. That's what he wanted them to do. He wanted them to do the kind of things that he had done—to meet needs that looked impossible, to set people free, to help them stand on their own two feet, to feed hungry people, to help others rise up out of the tombs that enslave them.

That is still our calling. We're expected to be miracle-workers, life-givers! In spite of our limitations, our poverty, our short supply of power when it comes to setting things right, we are called to be ministers in this world where we live. Sometimes we feel overwhelmed by it all. The problems are so huge and complex, and some seem so hopeless, and we think we don't have enough silver and gold to address the injustices and problems in our world. How can we perform miracles when we have so little to begin with? "Silver and gold—we don't have enough!" we want to cry out.

Well, let me suggest three simple things that emerge out of this story, three simple things we can all do to keep the song alive and going.

First, We Can Keep the Song Alive with Our Attention

Every time we give someone our undivided attention, every time we treat some human being with respect, the song goes on.

Notice the first thing Simon Peter did in Acts 3. He looked at the beggar, he saw him, he took notice of him. Most people long ago had stopped paying this man any attention. He blended into the landscape. Maybe they tossed a penny or two his way every now and then, but they paid him no mind. They didn't really see him. But Peter saw him that day, and he said to the man these interesting words: "Look at us" (verse 4). Peter looked at the man, and then he said to him, "Look at us."

Have you ever noticed how little eye contact there is between someone who is asking for a handout and the person being asked? There's a lot of self-consciousness involved, both in asking and giving. The one who is asking looks down; the passerby looks away. When Peter told the begging man to look at them, he was somehow subtly changing the whole relationship. He was giving him respect. He was giving him his attention. You know, we can give somebody money without giving that person our attention. In fact, there are times when money becomes a substitute for attention.

A man feels guilty for being so busy earning a living that he doesn't have time for his children. He leaves before they're up in the morning, and he comes home at night after they've gone to bed. He tries to make up for it with gifts, hoping that somehow they'll understand how much he really loves them. He doesn't find the time (or make the time) to get his wife a birthday present, so he tries to cover by giving her money and saying, "This is better. You can pick what you want." But deep down inside, he knows that what she really wants is a little thoughtfulness and a little attention.

A transient person comes to the church office asking for help. It's easier to give him a meal or bus fare to the next stop, than to have to listen to another long recital of woe. There are times when it's easier simply to give money. But when you give somebody your attention, you are giving something that everybody needs at one time or another. As Mother Teresa once put it, "I've come more and more to realize that it is being unwanted that is the worst disease any human being can ever experience, and unless there are willing hands to serve and loving hearts to love, this terrible disease can never be cured."

Through the power of the risen Christ, we can work miracles if we are willing to give attention. The song goes on when we give someone our undivided attention.

Second, We Can Keep the Song Alive with Our Understanding

Not long ago, I ran across one eight-year-old boy's definition of a grandmother. He said, "They are usually fat, but not too fat to tie up your shoelaces. They wear glasses, and sometimes they even take out their teeth. They can answer every hard question, like why dogs hate cats, and why God is not married. Everybody should try to have a grandmother, especially those who don't have television." The best thing about grandmothers is that they seem to understand. Maybe it's because they have been there. Somehow they know how you feel when you scrape your knee or when your best friend goes away or when you get in trouble and it doesn't seem fair. Everybody needs understanding.

As some of you know, our son Jeff has had a lot of knee injuries in his athletic career. Over the years he has had a number of knee surgeries. Some years ago we went again to the same hospital, the same floor, met the same surgical team and the same nurses. One male nurse was not our favorite. He was capable and efficient, but he seemed aloof, cold, tough, rough, uncaring, and unsympathetic. And when we checked into the hospital this time, wouldn't you know it, he was the first person we saw, and we all said out loud at the same time, "Oh, no! Not him again!" But surprisingly, this time he was a totally different person. He was tender, warm, gracious, helpful, caring, empathetic, and very understanding.

The morning we checked out, this nurse came by the room to help us, to say good-bye and to wish us well. I said to him,

"Thanks so much for all you've done for us. You are always good at your job, but you know, somehow you seem different, maybe more tender."

"Well," he said, "there's a good reason for that." Then, smiling broadly, he said, "I just got out of the hospital myself a week ago Friday. I spent seven days here as a patient. Now I know what that feels like. Now I know what a patient goes through, and I think it's made me more caring and more understanding."

The point is clear: People need understanding, and we become more understanding of them when we step into their shoes. Like Peter and John, we can (with the help of God) work miracles. We can give people new life if, in the spirit of Christ, we reach out to them with our attention, and with our understanding.

Third and Finally, We Can Keep the Song Alive with Our Love

Once I was teaching one of our Sunday school classes, and we were studying the parable of the prodigal son, and as we grappled with the meaning of that great story, my mind flashed back in time to something I hadn't thought of in years.

It happened in the early 1970s. Her name was Teresa. She was sixteen years old and having a hard time growing up. One Friday night she had an ugly fight with her parents. She ran away from home and stayed away for almost two years. Her parents searched for her desperately, but no luck. Finally, they hired a detective to find out where their daughter was and what she had been doing. The detective brought back a sordid story that I couldn't even begin to describe here. Teresa had done everything a girl could do that would break her parents' hearts. She had experimented with drugs and alcohol, had lived in a promiscuous commune, and had participated in all kinds of illicit activity.

Then one morning (it was Good Friday), the phone rang in my office. It was a collect call from Teresa. She was calling from San Francisco. She was crying. "Oh, Jim, I have done everything wrong! I have crushed my parents. I have hurt them so much. Now I realize how foolish I've been. I want to come home, but I don't know if Mom and Dad want me back. I wouldn't blame them if they didn't. I don't know how they could ever forgive me. I'm so sorry, and I want to come home!"

I told Teresa to go to the airport and to give her name at the airline desk. I would have a ticket home waiting there for her, and someone would be at the local airport to meet her plane.

When Teresa got off the plane on that Good Friday evening, she looked pretty rough. Her hair was dirty and matted. Her clothes were rumpled. Her eyes were tired and bloodshot. But her parents rushed to her and hugged her and welcomed her home with love and grace, crying tears of joy.

Two days later, on Easter Sunday morning, they were in church together. Teresa sat between her mother and father. She looked like a new person. She was radiant and beautiful. All through the service her parents kept touching her, patting her, hugging her. After the service, they came down to speak to me. As Teresa's mother hugged me tightly, she whispered in my ear, "Jim, I've always believed in the Resurrection, but never more than right now!"

Through the power of God's grace, we can work miracles when we, in the spirit of the risen Christ, reach out to others with attention, with understanding, and with love. When we do that, the song goes on—and we are part of it!

13. BRINGING OTHERS TO GOD

"He Couldn't Keep Jesus to Himself"

Scripture: John 6:1-14

There is a powerful story about the famous painter Albrecht Dürer that makes a significant point. The story is told to be true (but it may well be a legend). According to the story, Albrecht Dürer was one of eighteen children. The Dürer family lived in Nuremberg, Germany, in the fifteenth century. Albrecht and his brother, Albert, both wanted to become professional artists, but they had no money to pay their way through the art academy in Nuremberg. So they made a plan. Albert would work in the nearby mines and make money to support his brother through four years of the art school. And then Albrecht would work to pay for Albert's art training.

Albrecht went off to the art academy and did extremely ell. His artwork was outstanding (far better than the work of most of his professors), and by the time he graduated, he was beginning to earn large fees for hs commissioned works.

The plan was working well, but there was one thing the brothers had not counted on. During his four years in the mines, Albert had injured his hands repeatedly, and then arthritis has set in. His hands were so stiff that Albert could not hold a pen or brush in his right hand, much less draw or paint delicate lines on parchment or canvas.

In gratitude to Albert for his sacrificial love (and as a tribute to him), Albrecht Dürer created what has become his mos famous painting. It is known now all over the world as *The Praying Hands*. The hands in the painting are the injured hands of his brother, Albert, whose sacrifice had made Albrecht's career possible.

The next time you see a copy of this touching creation, take a second look; let it be a reminder that no one, no one, ever makes it alone!

Take Simon Peter, for example. He was one of the great leaders of the original disciples of Jesus. He was one of the great servants of the early church. He was one of the most beloved and respected saints in the history of the world, but he did not achieve that all by himself. The truth is, we are incredibly indebted to Simon Peter's brother, Andrew, for the gift of Peter to the church and to the world.

Andrew was the one who brought his brother, Simon Peter, into the presence of Jesus. Andrew was the one who encouraged Simon Peter. Andrew was the one who introduced Peter to Jesus. It's recorded in the first chapter of John's Gospel. Andrew finds the Messiah and then quickly runs to share the good news with his brother, Simon. The passage reads:

> One of the two who heard John speak and followed [Jesus] was Andrew, Simon Peter's brother. He first found his brother Simon and said to him, "We have found the Messiah" (which is translated *Anointed*). He brought Simon to Jesus. (John 1:40-42*a*)

In many ways, Andrew was an ordinary man. There is not much in the scriptures to distinguish him—at least not in the ways by which we usually measure greatness. So far as we know,

- Andrew performed no mighty deeds.
- He preached no great sermons.
- He did nothing extraordinary that we would classify as outstanding.
- He just served in his humble way.
- He just did what needed to be done without fanfare.
- No complaining, no griping, no questioning, no bellyaching, no jealousy.
- Andrew was too big for that kind of pettiness.

• To Andrew, all that mattered was to be with the Lord, to serve him as well as he could, and to bring others to him.

William Barclay, the prolific Bible scholar, wrote some remarkable words about Andrew some years ago. He said this:

> We do not possess a great deal of information about Andrew, but even the little that we know perfectly paints his character. He is one of the most attractive [characters] in the apostolic band [because] ... Andrew is characteristically the man who was always introducing others to Jesus. There are only three times in the gospel story when Andrew is brought into the center of the stage. There is this incident here, [in John 1] in which [Andrew] brings Peter to Jesus. There is the incident in John 6:8, 9 when he brings to Jesus the boy with the five loaves and two small fishes. And there is the incident in John 12:22 when he brings the inquiring Greeks into the presence of Jesus. It was Andrew's great joy to bring others to Jesus. He stands out as the man whose one desire was to share the glory. He is the man with the missionary heart. Having himself found the friendship of Jesus, he spent all his life in introducing others to that friendship. Andrew is our great example in that he could not keep Jesus to himself. (*The Gospel of John,* vol. 1, rev. ed., Philadelphia: Westminster Press, 1975, pp. 89-90)

Shaquille O'Neal is a professional basketball player in the NBA. He loves coming up with nicknames for himself. When he received his first Most Valuable Player award, Shaq gave himself a new nickname. He said that from that day on he wanted to be known as "the Big Aristotle" because Aristotle once said that excellence is not a singular act; it is a habit—you are what you repeatedly do.

Shaq was right, and Aristotle was right. Excellence is not one single act. It is found in what we repeatedly do well, and here is where we see the excellence of Andrew. He repeatedly introduced people to Jesus. He repeatedly brought people into the presence of Jesus. He repeatedly included people in the circle of his love and Christ's love.

This was the greatness of Andrew. He was so excited about what he had found in Christ that he couldn't sit still, he could not keep Jesus to himself. Let me show you what I mean.

First of All, Andrew Brought His Brother

The traffic officer was at his post directing traffic as usual. The intersection where he worked was a busy one. It was just in front of a large elementary school in the heart of the city. This caused the officer to be even more vigilant because he felt a keen responsibility (as he put it) "to look out after the little ones." His biggest fear was that one of the children might run out into the busy streets in front of a car or truck. And then one day it happened. A five-year-old student saw her mother on the other side of the street and ran right out in front of a car. The patrol officer saw it. He ran, diving toward the child. Stretched out full length, he gathered the little girl into his strong arms, hit the pavement hard, but protecting the child, he rolled to safety out of harm's way. The officer was scraped up a bit, but he had saved the life of the little girl.

When asked about his heroic effort, the officer said, "That's what we are here for, to take care of one another. That's what it's all about." He paused for a moment and then said, "Someone almost died today on my watch. No one dies on my beat!"

I suppose at that moment somewhere in heaven God was smiling because nothing pleases God more than to see us helping and serving one another, our sisters and brothers, in unselfish, sacrificial, self-giving ways.

Andrew found the Christ and immediately he ran to get his brother. This is a beautiful mountain-peak moment in the Bible. He brought his brother into the presence of Christ. Andrew's simple, thoughtful act of sharing with his brother is a poignant reminder to us that we in the world are not isolated individuals just existing alongside each other, selfishly hoarding whatever we can accumulate. No, we are family, and life is better when we act like a family, loving each other, supporting each other, helping each other, respecting each other, treasuring each other, and, like Andrew, bringing each other into the presence of Christ and the circle of Christ's love.

I have been reading Coach Mike Krzyzewski's book, *Leading with the Heart* (New York, Warner Books, 2000). Coach K, as he is known, is the highly successful men's basketball coach at Duke University who has led his team to back-to-back national championships in 1991 and 1992, a third national championship in 2001, and nine Final Four appearances since 1986. In his book, Coach K speaks out of his own experiences and what he had learned about leadership in basketball, business, and life. His philosophy at Duke is very simple, but very profound. In essence, he says to his team: "We are a family, so love one another, help one another, support one another. We are a family, so use plural pronouns. It's not about 'me,' it's about 'us,' and what we can do together. Don't do anything detrimental to our family." If two freshmen oversleep and miss the team bus, he doesn't just deal with the two freshmen, he deals with the whole team. Why didn't someone miss them? Why didn't someone check on them? Why didn't someone wake them up? If one of them is late, all of them are late! What happens to one of them happens to all of them because they are a family (pp. 10-12).

Isn't that a great philosophy for a basketball team, and for a church? We learn it from Andrew! It is our responsibility, our privilege, our joy to bring our brothers and our sisters into the presence of Christ.

That's number one: Andrew brought his brother.

Second, Andrew Brought a Child

One day Jesus was on the mountain teaching a huge throng of people. Jesus realized that the people were hungry. The disciples' immediate response was to say to Jesus, "Lord, send them away. Shut this down. Let them fend for themselves. Let them find their own food. Tell them to go home." That's what all of the disciples said; all, that is, except Andrew. Andrew went out and found a young boy who had brought his lunch. The boy had a little bread and two fish. Andrew, with great faith, brought the boy to Jesus, and in the hands of Jesus this small amount of food became enough to feed the whole crowd (see John 6:1-14).

Andrew's act reminds us dramatically of how important children and their resources are to Christ and his church. Andrew's act shows us graphically how crucial it is for us in our words and deeds to bring children into the presence of Jesus.

There is a legend that comes out of Missouri that makes the point powerfully. According to the story, many years ago in Missouri, a minister made a bad mistake in moral judgment that later came back to haunt him and to hurt many others. Through trickery, conniving, and scheming, the minister stole a man's dog. That's bad enough, but to make matters worse, he included his two little boys in the deception. The two boys helped their father disguise the dog so that the rightful owner could not claim him. The boys enjoyed the trickery and plotting. The boys thought it was great fun to take away the man's dog.

Some years later, the minister realized that in that one deceitful act, he had taught his sons how to steal and turned them away from the Christlike spirit of love and kindness and goodness and respect for others. And, he said, regretfully, "It was a terrible mistake on my part. I was able to keep the dog, but I lost my sons."

Oh, by the way, the names of those two little boys were Frank and Jesse James! They grew up to become two of the most notorious outlaws and robbers of the Old West. Their minister dad never forgave himself.

That's a dramatic example, to be sure. But it is true, so true, that our children do indeed watch us closely and learn so much from what we do.

How do we bring our children to Christ? By getting them involved in church and Sunday school and youth activities, by telling them the stories of Jesus, by introducing them to the power of the scriptures, by teaching them to pray, by leading them to understand that some things are right to do and some things are wrong; but even more, by letting them see us loving Christ, serving the church, and living the faith every day with heart, soul, mind, and strength.

This is what we learn from Andrew—to bring our brothers and sisters to Christ, and to bring our children to Christ.

Third and Finally, Andrew Brought the Inquiring Greeks to Christ

That is, he brought into the presence of Christ some people who were very different from him.

Do you remember the old TV show *Green Acres*? It was about a city slicker, New York lawyer named Oliver Wendell Douglas, and his wife, Lisa, who left the big city behind to be farmers near Hooterville. Hooterville had a marching band made up of Sam Drucker, who ran the general store; and Uncle Joe, whose niece Kate ran the Shady Rest Hotel; and, of course, Arnold Ziffel, the pig, was also in the band. Oliver Douglas was the band director. But no matter what song he selected or what song he directed, they always played "There'll Be a Hot Time in the Old Town Tonight," because that was the only song they knew!

This reminds me of the people in the time of Jesus. They had only known one "song" when it came to other people. They had been taught to love, but they were taught to love *only* those who looked like them, talked like them, dressed like them, acted like them, and ate like them, and everybody else was seen as an enemy, an adversary, and a threat.

But then along came Jesus to be the Savior of all people, and he taught that we should love everybody, even those different from us, even those called our enemies. It was a new song, a needed song, a great song that still needs to be sung today, the song of inclusive love, gracious love, compassionate love, accepting love, unconditional love. And the question is, have we learned to sing it?

Andrew had learned it well, and he sang it boldly by bringing people, all sorts of people, into the presence of Jesus Christ. He brought his brother, he brought a child, and he brought the Greeks, people different from him.

Let me ask you something. How long has it been since you brought somebody into the presence of Christ?

14. MARRIAGE AND GOD

"Celebrating the Gift of Marriage"

Scripture: John 13:34-35

They said it couldn't be done. They said it was physically impossible. They said it would never happen, but on May 6, 1954, a young medical student named Roger Bannister did it: He ran a mile in under four minutes!

For centuries, as far back as the Olympic games in ancient Greece, it was believed that the human being could not break the four-minute mile. It was determined by medical doctors and physiologists that the human body was so constructed that it would be physically impossible to run a mile in less than four minutes. Our bone structure was simply all wrong. The wind resistance was too great. Our lung capacity was inadequate to accomplish this amazing feat. There was just one problem with that conclusion. They forgot to tell Roger Bannister—or at least they didn't convince him.

And so at the Iffley Road Track in Oxford on a wet and windy day on May 6, 1954, with 3,000 people watching, Great Britain's Roger Bannister did the unthinkable. He ran the mile in 3 minutes, 59.4 seconds and in the process established a new world record—a record that lasted, interestingly, only forty-six days.

Forty-six days later, John Landy of Australia lowered the record to 3.58. The astonishing thing is that after Roger Bannister broke the four-minute mile barrier, thirty-seven other runners accomplished it in the months that followed. Since that time 955 runners have done it. Just nine years after Roger Bannister's historic run, Jim Ryun accomplished a sub-four minute while still in high school.

As of this writing, the current world record holder is Hicham el-Guerrouj of Morocco. He ran the mile in about 3 minutes, 43 seconds, and at that pace he would have finished 120 yards ahead of Roger Bannister.

They said it couldn't be done, but once one runner did it, the sub-four-minute mile became a rather commonplace occurrence in the world of track and field. For example, John McDonnell is the track coach at the University of Arkansas. In his years of coaching, more than twenty of his runners have broken the four-minute mile.

Now, what does this have to do with us today? Just this: It shows us dramatically that when people believe something can be done, when people know that something can be done, it opens the door of possibility for them. It raises the bar of their expectation, and rather than to say, "It can't be done," they say, "I can do that, too."

With this in mind, let me tell you that in our church family right now, we have 126 couples who have been married for fifty years or longer. Of these 126 couples, 28 of the couples have been married for over sixty years. The point is, it can be done, and when we know that it's doable, then we can with more confidence strive to accomplish that feat.

Now, let me hurry to say what we all know, that there are some situations that somehow become so painful, so destructive, and sometimes even so dangerous that the only answer is to dissolve the relationship, to learn from that and move on and make a new beginning with your life. And if that happens, you can know that God loves you and God is with you, and that the church is here with incredible resources to support you and encourage you and to help you shape a new beginning.

But apart from those hurtful situations, it is doable; couples can make it work. The key word here is *work*. We have to work at it. As someone once said, "Good marriages are made in heaven, but they have to be worked out here on earth."

So let me share some ideas with you about this. Over the years I have visited with many, many married couples, some happy and some not so happy; and I have learned through those conversations and experiences that there are certain predictable, insidious, negative things that can sour the relationship and poison the marriage. These same problems crop up over and over again, and the bottom line is that we are better off not doing these things.

So, here they are. If you want to have a happy, healthy marriage and a joyful relationship, here are three things you need to avoid like the plague, three things NOT to do!

First of All, Don't Be Crabby

In the "Peanuts" cartoon, Lucy is Queen of Crabbiness. She loves to rain on other people's parades. Once, her little brother, Linus, drew a cartoon. He was so proud of it. He wanted Lucy to look at it and compliment it and be proud of him. She said, "Who drew it?" Linus said, "I drew it." And Lucy said, "If you drew it, then I think it's terrible!" Dejected, Linus walked away, saying, "Big sisters are the crabgrass in the lawn of life!"

Lucy *always* pulls the football away and causes Charlie Brown to fall on his back. She *always* gripes and complains. She is *always* crabby. Now, it may be funny in Charles Schulz's classic and beloved comic strip, but you wouldn't want to be married to Lucy. It's not fun to be around crabby people.

Now, let me hurry to say that crabbiness is no respecter of genders. Men can be crabby, and women can be crabby. But as Christians we should not be crabby!

Christianity is by definition "responsive gratitude." As Christians we are grateful to God for the gift of life, and grateful to God for the incredible gift of eternal and abundant life that we have because of the sacrificial love of Jesus Christ. Gratitude, appreciation, thankfulness, joy, love, kindness, graciousness, tenderness, compassion, humility—these are key marks of the Christian. Not grouchiness.

But unfortunately, sometimes we forget that, and we give in to anger and cynicism and pessimism and selfishness. And when that happens, we can become grumpy and crabby, and then our prevailing spirit is to fuss and gripe and complain about everything.

Some years ago a young pastor in Scotland was sent to a new church. Now, there was a woman in that church named Mrs. McTavish, who seemed to have been born in an objective mood. She was against everything. She never agreed with anybody on anything. She was stubborn and harsh and bitter about everything, and she seemed always to be in a bad mood.

One Sunday morning, she and the young pastor clashed. Hard words were spoken. Later, the young pastor felt sorry and sad. He had said some things he regretted. So he went to Mrs. McTavish's home to apologize and to ask for her forgiveness.

As the pastor approached her apartment, he saw Mrs. McTavish looking out the window, so he knew she was at home. He went up to the door and rang the bell. No response. He knocked on the door. No response. He knocked louder and called out her name. Still, no response.

He then proceeded to do something no minister should ever do. He stooped down on one knee and looked through the keyhole. Well, it just so happened that Mrs. McTavish had done the same thing on her side of the door at the same time. As their eyes met through the keyhole, the young minister said, "Well, well, Mrs. McTavish, this is the first time that you and I have seen eye-to-eye on anything!"

Then Mrs. McTavish opened the door and did something the minister had never seen her do before: She smiled! And then she laughed loudly. The young pastor laughed with her and asked for forgiveness. She took his hand warmly and invited him in for tea. She said she was sorry, too, and that she didn't mean to be so cantankerous. Then she said, "I guess I'm just lonely. You are the first person to come to see me since my husband died more than ten years ago."

The point is, Mrs. McTavish had not always been crabby. She had become overwhelmed by her problems, and in the process, she lost her gratitude, she lost her joy, she lost her sense of humor. Please don't let that happen to you. If you feel disillusioned with life, get help. The gift of life and love is too precious to waste in crabbiness.

Some years ago, I was working with a middle-aged couple who were having serious marriage problems. One day in my office, the wife said to her husband: "I don't see why you have to talk so ugly to me. No matter what I say, you react with hostility, and you put me down with hateful angry words."

"Aw, honey," he said, "you know how I am. It's just talk. I'm just blowing off steam. I don't mean anything by it. You understand that, don't you?"

And she said: "No, I don't understand that. I will never understand that. When you talk to me that way, it breaks my heart! How can you love me and speak to me with such hostile hatefulness?

Time after time over the years I have seen it—that crabby, grumpy attitude tearing marriages apart. So, that's number one: Don't be crabby! Be grateful!

Second, Don't Be Critical

Especially, don't be *contemptuously* critical, and don't give advice. As someone once said, "Don't give advice. Wise folks don't need it; fools won't heed it!"

We only have so much breath, so why not use that breath to form words that build people up instead of words that tear people down?

In French, the word *encourage* literally means "to put the heart in." The word *discourage* means "to tear the heart out." In the Christian home, we should go overboard in saying words that encourage and affirm and reassure, not words that tear people down.

All my life I have heard this advice: "A good thing to remember and a better thing to do, is to work with the construction gang, and not with the wrecking crew."

The truth is that all of us have way too many faults of our own to be harshly and arrogantly and contemptuously critical of others. We all have sinned and fallen short of the glory of God. Besides that, it is so much more rewarding, so much more loving, and so much more fun to encourage your loved ones than to cut them down with critical words or contemptuous body language and actions that wound and devastate and break the heart.

A famous minister had a two o'clock appointment with a man he had never met before. The man wanted counseling. When the minister returned from lunch at 1:45, he received an emergency call about a death in the church family. He took the call as he should have, but it made him four minutes late for his two o'clock counseling appointment. When the minister walked into the counseling office, the man immediately took him to task. "You are four minutes late for our appointment," the man said. "Let me give you a little advice. Be on time. It was rude of you to keep me waiting like this."

The minister apologized and asked for forgiveness for his tardiness, and then the minister asked, "How may I be of service to you?" And the man said, "I have trouble sustaining a relationship. People don't seem to enjoy being around me for some reason." The minister measured his words and said, "Well, you know, you and I had never met until today, and you were pretty harsh with me because I was a few minutes late. I didn't tell you before, but the reason I was late was because I had an emergency call. A good friend's mother just died, and I was trying to help her, and the call took a little longer than I had anticipated. People don't enjoy being fussed at or criticized, and maybe that's why they pull away from you. It's always best to be gracious. It's always best to cut people a little slack. It's always best to be kind. It's always best to be loving."

That minister was right, wasn't he?

So, if you want a love relationship that will mature and grow and sustain and deepen; if you want it to be fun and joyful and tender and beautiful, then first, don't be crabby (be grateful); and second, don't be critical (be respectful).

Third and Finally, Don't Be Controlling

In a marriage, it is so important, so crucial to remember that you don't always have to be in charge; that you don't always have to be in control; that you don't always have to make every decision.

That's the beauty of marriage. It's a shared relationship, a shared wisdom, a shared love. Sometimes people forget that, and they try to take control. Their motto is "My way or the highway." They don't even realize that in so doing, they are implying to their mate, "I'm smarter than you," "I don't trust your judgment," "I don't think you have a lick of sense." And that is not the Christian spirit.

It is so important to keep the courtship alive in a marriage, and this control tactic is a great enemy of love and courtship. Society plays a terrible trick on us here. During the early courtship, the engagement, the wedding, and the honeymoon, society smiles and says, "Isn't that sweet? Look at that great couple—so in love. Isn't that wonderful?"

But then, here's the trick. After the honeymoon, society turns on us and says, "No, no, no! Don't be too sweet to each other; you might get henpecked. Don't be too sweet to each other; you might lose control of your life!"

I heard a psychologist talking about this on TV. She summed it up like this: "During the courtship, I was scared to death that I was going to lose him. After the honeymoon, I was scared to death I was going to lose me."

What's the answer? Simply this: Keep the courtship alive by getting up in the morning and going to bed at night thinking, *How can I bring joy and happiness and pleasure and support to this life-mate of mine that I love so much?* If you have two people doing that at the same time, you have heaven on earth.

Once I ran across an article on marriage in a magazine. It was pretty routine, but it had one great line in it that touched my soul. The article said: "If you ever find yourself in a situation where you can either make yourself look good or your mate look good, *always choose to make your mate look good.*"

That is so true—and so Christian. Now, you may be wondering when I'm going to get to our biblical text for this chapter, so here it comes. In John 13:34, Jesus said, "I give you a new commandment, that you love one another. Just as I have loved you, you also should love one another."

Notice now that Jesus did not just say, "Love one another." He said, "Love one another, as I have loved you." That is the key to a great Christian marriage—two people loving each other in the way Christ loved, generously, graciously, compassionately, sacrificially, unconditionally. That's the way to make a marriage work and last and be joyful and celebrative, to love each other with a Christlike spirit, with a Christlike love.

One morning a Sunday school teacher told her fifth-graders the story of Jesus' first miracle. It happened at a wedding in Cana of Galilee. After the teacher finished telling the story, she asked her class, "Now, what do we learn from this story?" A little boy raised his hand and said, "I learned that when you have a wedding, it's a good idea to have Jesus there!"

Indeed so! And when you have a marriage, it's a good idea to have Jesus there because Jesus reminds us

not to be crabby, but to be grateful;
not to be critical, but to be respectful;
not to be controlling, but to be gracious.

15. PURPOSE IN GOD

"The Power of a Purpose"

Scripture: Matthew 6:25-33

A couple of years ago when our son, Jeff, was in college, he went through a frustrating period in which he was constantly losing his keys. He could not for the life of him keep up with his keys. This was in part caused by the fact that college guys these days often wear clothes with no pockets. They live in gym shorts or those jogging sweatsuits with elastic around the waist and the ankles, but no pockets. So Jeff was forever losing his keys.

To help out, we bought him one of those battery-operated "key-finders." Have you seen those? You attach your keys to this electronic key-ring gadget. And then when you clap your hands four times to the rhythm of "one-potato, two-potato, three-potato, four," the little key-finder will chirp eight times like a cricket, and following the sound, you can find your keys.

Well, we got one of those for Jeff, and he loved it. He became the hit of the college campus. Everywhere he went, people would clap four times to hear the crickets chirp. This went over especially well in the college library!

However, one weekend when Jeff came home for a visit, he and I went to the grocery store one Saturday morning, and something in the electronic cash register set off the key-finder. As we stood there in line together at the grocery store, it began chirping incessantly like a cricket in his pocket. I did what any good father would do in a moment like that: I acted like I didn't know him!

However, it does bring up an interesting point, doesn't it, namely this: Sometimes we do need help in finding the key—the key to life! That's what I want us to think about together. One of the most essential and dramatic keys to zestful living is having a sense of purpose. There is great power in that. Let me show you what I mean.

One evening, a few weeks ago, I was feeling terrible. My head was throbbing. My stomach was in knots. I was physically worn out and completely exhausted, emotionally drained. I prescribed for myself a nap on the couch in the den. My head had just touched the pillow when the phone rang. A voice on the line gave me the bad news that one of our most devoted church members (and a very close personal friend) had just died. His wife was still at the hospital, in shock. She needed help. Could I go?

I was up and going out of the door in less than five minutes. And amazingly, as I drove toward the hospital, I made a surprising discovery: Suddenly my headache was gone, and the internal queasiness I had felt so dramatically only moments before had completely subsided. I didn't feel tired or weak anymore. I felt a deep sadness over the loss of a good friend. I felt love and compassion for his wife and family, who had so suddenly been thrust into a state of shock and into the valley of grief.

But in my concern to help, and in my intense desire to be a friend and a pastor, I had been forced by the situation to get outside myself, and as a result, all of my ailments that had seemed so severe and so taxing just brief minutes earlier had literally gone away! Isn't that incredible? Some people would call that "instant recovery." Others might call it a "second wind." Still others would call it "overcoming self-pity." But I would call it "the power of a purpose," for you see, a sense of purpose gives us power to do things we never dreamed possible!

For example, some years ago I read in a newspaper a story about a woman in Kentucky who pulled a 2,000-pound car off of her little boy after they had plunged off the highway into a ditch. "He was pinned under the car," the woman said, "and I didn't even think about how heavy the car was. I just knew I had to get it off him, so I did!" Some people would call that "hysterical strength" or "adrenaline might," but I would call it "the power of a purpose."

Two women entered the hospital on the same day and had the

same operation. It took one of them a full year to recuperate, and all through the year she complained about how much she was suffering. The other woman was up and going strong, working, washing, cooking, and all the rest, within ten days! It took one of them a full year to recover and the other only ten days. Why? What was the difference? Well, the difference is found in the fact that the woman who got well so quickly *had to*—she had three preschool children at home to care for! Once again we see it, "the power of a purpose"!

J. Wallace Hamilton, in his book *Where Now Is Thy God?* speaks eloquently of how a sense of purpose can give us incredible power (Old Tappan, N.J., Fleming H. Revell Co., 1969, pp. 33-35). He strings together three fascinating statements.

First a statement by a medical doctor at the University of Vienna: "There is nothing in the world which helps us surmount our difficulties, survive our disasters or which keeps us healthy and happy as the knowledge of a life task worthy of our devotion...." A PURPOSE! We cannot advance in life with any buoyancy, unless we are sure that where we are going has destination—and what we are doing has meaning. Purpose in life is the Savior of life.

A second statement is from one of George Moore's novels, in which he tells of Irish peasants in the period of the Great Depression, put to work by the government in building roads. For a time, the men worked well, sang their Irish songs, glad to be back at work again and they were very productive. But little by little, they discovered that the roads they were building led nowhere. They just ran out into dreary bogs and stopped.

As the truth gradually dawned on them that they had been put to work solely to provide them employment and as an excuse the government could have for feeding them, the men grew listless and stopped singing, and their productivity fell off. Commenting on the incident, the author (George Moore) said: "The roads to nowhere are difficult to make. For a person to work well and sing ... there must be an end in view." It's so important to have a purpose!

The third statement comes from the Old Testament. It's found in the grand old story of Nehemiah rebuilding the broken walls of Jerusalem. It seemed such a hopeless task, with the walls in ruins, the people scattered, and everyone so discouraged and despondent, scared and disillusioned. And all around were enemies who wanted no strong Jerusalem and were doing everything in their power to prevent it. They tried ridicule first, then persuasion. They scoffed, they taunted, they criticized, they threatened! But Nehemiah went right on with his work as though he didn't know they were there. Four times the threat went up, and four times the answer from Nehemiah came back, "Shall such a man as I flee? I am doing a great work, and I cannot come down!" Isn't it refreshing here in this Old Testament passage to find a man so committed to a purpose that nothing can discourage him, no criticism can distract him, no side issue can pull him away! The power of a purpose. "I'm doing a great work and I cannot come down!"

Nehemiah's single-minded commitment here reminds me of Roy Smith's famous story of the bulldog. He met this bulldog on a narrow path one day. The bulldog never slowed down, never hesitated, never veered to the right or to the left. The bulldog just kept right on walking with eyes straightforward, until Roy Smith had to jump out of the way and let him pass. As the bulldog walked by, Roy Smith said a simple prayer: "O Lord, give me just a little bit of what that bulldog has a whole lot of!"

Purpose, commitment, single-mindedness, dedication to a great cause—whatever you want to call it, that is what gives meaning to life! It's the fiber of Christianity! But what is our purpose? Jesus helps us here. In fact, that is why he came, to show us the purpose of life, to show us what God wants us to do and be. He put it like this in the Sermon on the Mount: "The purpose of life is to seek first the kingdom of God and his righteousness, and everything then falls into place for you" (Matthew 6:33, paraphrase). In other words, he was saying, "Listen, dedicate your life to serving God, and then trust him to bring it all out right."

On another occasion Jesus said, "Your real purpose in life is to love God and to love people" (Matthew 22:37-39, paraphrase).

Just do that; commit your life to doing that, and your life will be full and rich and zestful and meaningful because you will be in harmony with God's purpose, and that purpose will give you *power* for the living of these days.

Let me show you what I mean. Look with me at some of the ways purpose can give us power.

First, Purpose Gives Us the Power to See Problems as Opportunities

We see this dramatically in Nehemiah. He saw a "run-down" Jerusalem not just as a problem, but as an opportunity for him to do something great for God and God's people. Nehemiah could easily have given up, thrown up his hands, and said, "It's no use; Jerusalem is done for! Israel has had it!" But no, rather, he said, "I will rebuild the city!" You see, if you know your purpose, it gives you the eyes of faith to see problems as opportunities.

There's a story about two shoe salesmen who were sent to a remote country to open up a new market there. Three days after their arrival, the first salesman sent a cablegram that read: "Returning home on next plane. Can't possibly sell shoes here. Everybody goes barefoot!" Nothing was heard from the second salesman for about two weeks. Then came a fat airmail envelope with this message for the home office: "Fifty orders enclosed! Many more to come! Prospects unlimited! Great opportunity! Nobody here has shoes!"

Purpose gives us the power to see problems as opportunities!

Second, Purpose Gives Us the Power to Rise Above the Fear of Criticism

Any time we do something responsible, any time we try to give leadership, any time we take a stand, we open ourselves to criticism. Nehemiah came back to Jerusalem, and he began to rebuild the walls of that great ancient city. As he worked, he became the object of great criticism. His enemies taunted him, they made fun of him, they whispered behind his back, they ridiculed him, they laughed at him, they criticized him mercilessly, they threatened him cruelly. But Nehemiah kept right on working, and he answered, "Should such a man as I flee? I'm doing a great work and I cannot come down!" (See Nehemiah 6:3, 11.)

During the War Between the States, President Abraham Lincoln was criticized slanderously, scathingly, by both sides, but he was committed to saving the Union. He had a great purpose, and he said, "If I were to try to read, much less answer, all the attacks made on me, this [office] might as well be closed for any other business. I do the very best I know how—the very best I can; and I mean to keep doing so until the end.... If the end brings me out wrong, ten angels swearing I was right would make no difference" (*The Inner Life of Abraham Lincoln: Six Months at the White House* by Francis B. Carpenter, Lincoln, University of Nebraska Press, 1995, pp. 258-59). Lincoln was committed to a great purpose, and that gave him the power to rise above the fear of criticism. Like Nehemiah before him, he was saying, "You can criticize me if you must, but I am doing a great work, and I cannot come down!"

Third, Purpose Gives Us the Power to Live Meaningfully

When we have a sense of purpose, it makes us happy, productive, and whole. Our lives become zestful, creative, and meaningful. I am convinced that what people want and need more than anything else is meaning in their lives, a sense of mission, a great dream, an urgent cause, a commitment that really matters, a destination.

Remember that fascinating slice of dialogue in *Alice in Wonderland*:

Alice (speaking to the cat): "Would you
  please tell me which way I ought
  to go from here?"
Cat: "That depends a good deal on
  where you want to go."
Alice: "Oh, I don't much care."

Cat: "Then it doesn't really matter
  which way you go."
Alice: "But I want to go somewhere."
Cat: "Oh, you are sure to do that!"

Many people drift through life with no sense of direction and miss their meaning, never find their purpose, and they come up empty-handed, frustrated, depressed, and ashamed. I wonder if you and I will come to the end of our lives ashamed because we never found our way, our mission, our unique purpose.

The purpose of life, according to Jesus, is to seek God's kingdom, to love God, and to love people. Anything less is not worth much! If you know your purpose, it makes life meaningful and zestful and joyous.

Finally, Purpose Gives Us the Power to See the Routine, Mundane, and Commonplace as Sacred

Oh, how Jesus could do this! Think about him for a moment. Remember Jesus' appreciation of little things—brooms, candles, water, leaven, old cloth, flowers, birds, seeds, sunsets, wind, and the grass of the fields. They were holy to Jesus. They were sacred to him because they spoke to him of the Father!

I'm a real fan of the *Peanuts* comic strip, with Charlie Brown. One of my all-time favorites is the one where Charlie Brown, Linus, and Lucy are lying on their backs on a hill, looking at the clouds. Lucy says, "If you use your imagination, you can see lots of things in the cloud formations. What do you think you see, Linus?"

Linus replies, "Well, those clouds up there look to me like the map of the British Honduras on the Caribbean. That cloud up there looks a little like the profile of Thomas Eakins, the famous painter and sculptor. And that group of clouds over there gives me the impression of the stoning of Stephen. I can see the apostle Paul standing there to one side."

Lucy says, "Uh huh. That's very good. What do YOU see in the clouds, Charlie Brown?"

And Charlie Brown says, "Well, I was going to say I saw a ducky and a horsie, but I changed my mind!"

We can all relate to Charlie Brown, can't we? There are so many things out there to see and we don't always see them. But when we find our great dream, our unique mission, our special cause, our real purpose, then everything speaks to us of God. We become "sermonic bloodhounds" sniffing out God's truth everywhere. Every bush becomes a "burning bush." Every place becomes a sacred place. Everywhere we look, everything we see reminds us of God and all that he has lovingly prepared for us.

If we know our purpose, we have power to see problems as opportunities, to rise above criticism, to find meaning in life, and to see the sacred even in the most commonplace things.

SUGGESTIONS FOR LEADING A STUDY OF

There's a Hole in Your Soul That Only God Can Fill

John D. Schroeder

This book by James W. Moore shows readers how to fill their hearts and souls with God's love by seeking first God's kingdom and placing God at the center of their lives. To assist you in facilitating a discussion group, this study guide was created to help make this experience beneficial for both you and members of your group. Here are some thoughts on how you can help your group:

1. Distribute the book to participants before your first meeting and request that they come having read the first chapter. You may want to limit the size of your group to increase participation.
2. Begin your sessions on time. Your participants will appreciate your promptness. You may wish to begin your first session with introductions and a brief get-acquainted time. Start each session by reading aloud the snapshot summary of the chapter for the day.
3. Select discussion questions and activities in advance. Note that the first question is a general question designed to get discussion going. The last question is designed to summarize the discussion. Feel free to change the order of the listed questions and to create your own questions. Allow a set amount of time for the questions and activities.
4. Remind your participants that all questions are valid as part of the learning process. Encourage their participation in discussion by saying that there are no "wrong" answers and that all input will be appreciated. Invite participants to share their thoughts, personal stories, and ideas as their comfort level allows.
5. Some questions may be more difficult to answer than others. If you

ask a question and no one responds, begin the discussion by venturing an answer yourself. Then ask for comments and other answers. Remember that some questions may have multiple answers.

6. Ask the question "Why?" or "Why do you believe that?" to help continue a discussion and give it greater depth.

7. Give everyone a chance to talk. Keep the conversation moving. Occasionally you may want to direct a question to a specific person who has been quiet. "Do you have anything to add?" is a good follow-up question to ask another person. If the topic of conversation gets off track, move ahead by asking the next question in your study guide.

8. Before moving from questions to activities, ask group members if they have any questions that have not been answered. Remember that as a leader, you do not have to know all the answers. Some answers may come from group members. Other answers may even need a bit of research. Your job is to keep the discussion moving and to encourage participation.

9. Review the activity in advance. Feel free to modify it or to create your own activity. Encourage participants to try the "At home" activity.

10. Following the conclusion of the activity, close with a brief prayer, praying either the printed prayer from the study guide or a prayer of your own. If your group desires, pause for individual prayer petitions.

11. Be grateful and supportive. Thank group members for their ideas and participation.

12. You are not expected to be a "perfect" leader. Just do the best you can by focusing on the participants and the lesson. God will help you lead this group.

13. Enjoy your time together!

Suggestions for Participants

1. What you will receive from this study will be in direct proportion to your involvement. Be an active participant!

2. Please make it a point to attend all sessions and to arrive on time so that you can receive the greatest benefit.

3. Read the chapter and review the study guide questions prior to the meeting. You may want to jot down questions you have from the reading, and also answers to some of the study guide questions.

4. Be supportive and appreciative of your group leader as well as the other members of your group. You are on a journey together.

5. Your participation is encouraged. Feel free to share your thoughts about the material being discussed.

6. Pray for your group and your leader.

Introduction

"My Soul Is Restless, O God, 'Til It Finds Its Rest in Thee"

Snapshot Summary

1. Recognize boredom for what it really is: a symptom of inner emptiness.

2. See time as a precious gift from God.

3. Get "outside" yourself.

Reflection / Discussion Questions

1. What interests you in this topic? Share what you hope to gain from reading this book and participating in this study.

2. What feelings are associated with being bored? How do you know when you are bored?

3. List some of the ways boredom causes damage to us.

4. Explain how boredom is more of a symptom than a problem.

5. Share a time when you experienced trouble because you were bored.

6. Give some reasons why time is a precious gift from God.

7. How and why does time get wasted?

8. Reflect on / discuss ways that we can use our time wisely.

9. Explain how you get "outside" yourself.

10. Why is love a good antidote for boredom?

11. Why does self-centeredness cause boredom? Give an example.

12. What are you going to do the next time you feel bored?

Activities

As a group: Create a poster listing or illustrating boredom busters. Hang it in the classroom or in a church hallway.

At home: Reflect on the precious gift of time. How can you use this gift more effectively? Name a time-management strength and weakness you have.

Prayer: *Dear God, thank you for the precious gift of time. Help us use it wisely and recognize boredom as a symptom of emptiness we feel when our lives aren't centered on you. Grant us the ability to make the life changes we need in order to be more effective in loving you and serving others. Open our eyes to our faults and show us our potential. Amen.*

Chapter 1

Faith in God

"Got My Own"

Snapshot Summary
1. We need our own faith.
2. We need our own hope.
3. We need our own love.

Reflection / Discussion Questions
1. Who first shared their faith with you? How did you learn about Jesus?
2. What message was Paul trying to convey in this passage of Philippians 2:12-13?
3. List some of the different ways in which faith gets shared.
4. What does it mean to have your own faith? Why is this important?
5. Share a time when you were sent help that you did not expect.
6. What is *hope*? Give your own definition.
7. Why are Christians people of hope?
8. How can we pass on hope to others?

9. Why do we need our own love?

10. How does Jesus want us to love? List some ways.

11. Name some keys to loving one another that you have learned over the years.

12. How can God help us grow in faith, hope, and love?

Activities

As a group: Create a "Got My Own Faith / Hope / Love" bookmark for your Bibles.

At home: Share your faith with someone this week.

Prayer: *Dear God, thank you for the gifts of faith, hope, and love. Help us accept these gifts in our own lives, and then pass them on to others. Show us how to be loving servants. Help us pray more often and work harder to further your kingdom. May we bring joy and peace to others by working to change the world, one person at a time. Amen.*

Chapter 2

Trust in God

"Have You Ever Run Out of Gas?"

Snapshot Summary

1. Come what may, keep on trusting God wholeheartedly.

2. Come what may, keep on performing the holy habits regularly.

3. Come what may, keep on loving other people sacrificially.

Reflection / Discussion Questions

1. What causes us to "run out of gas" spiritually?

2. Explain what it means to trust God. What sometimes prevents us from trusting in God?

3. Give a summary of what Paul expressed in Philippians 3:12-16.

4. How important are goals? What is your experience with goal-setting in your life?

5. Share a time when you quit something and later had regrets about it.

6. What is a *habit*? Explain the difference between a good habit and a bad one.

7. List the "holy habits" that feed and fuel our souls.

8. Compare the benefits and the costs of maintaining holy habits.

9. Explain the meaning of *sacrificial love*.

10. How did Jesus show us the meaning of sacrificial love?

11. Name some acts or examples of sacrificial love.

12. What are you going to do the next time you feel you are spiritually running out of gas?

Activities

As a group: Provide each person with a 3-by-5-inch card to create a symbol to place somewhere in their cars as a reminder to "gas up" spiritually.

At home: Reflect on your habits, and work on strengthening your "holy habits."

Prayer: *Dear God, thank you for the gift of trust. Help us trust you and remember that you always know what is best. Help us trust our friends and family when we need advice and direction. Remind us of the importance of holy habits so that our souls continue to be fed. And may we strive to love others sacrificially and follow the example of our Lord. Amen.*

Chapter 3

Excitement in God

"I've Got a Strong Case of the 'Can't Help Its'"

Snapshot Summary

1. Christians can't help but be grateful.
2. Christians can't help but be confident.
3. Christians can't help but be loving.

Reflection / Discussion Questions

1. Describe the apostle Andrew's enthusiasm for Jesus. Why was he so excited?
2. How do you catch a case of the "can't help its"; what is the key?
3. Explain the meaning of *responsive gratitude*.
4. Share a memory of a time when you were very grateful.
5. What feelings are associated with gratefulness?
6. How can we show our gratitude to God?
7. Explain what it means to have confidence in Christ.
8. Share something that you are confident about.
9. What has knowing Jesus taught you about love?
10. Share a time when you were the recipient of Christian love.
11. What motivates a person to want to share Jesus with others?
12. What's so exciting about the Christian life?

Activities

As a group: List seven more wonders of the world in addition to those already listed in this chapter.

At home: Share your excitement in God by inviting someone to attend church with you next Sunday.

Prayer: *Dear God, thank you for the power of excitement and enthusiasm. Help us not only want to share you with others, but also go to great lengths to do so. You are an awesome God, and everyone needs to know it. Help us be grateful, confident, and loving as we live our lives, that we may touch the lives of others. Amen.*

Chapter 4

Disciples of God

"Dear Hope, Keep Living Up to Your Name"

Snapshot Summary

1. We live up to our name as Christians when we live with Christlike commitment.

2. We live up to our name as Christians when we live with Christlike character.

3. We live up to our name as Christians when we live with Christlike compassion.

Reflection / Discussion Questions

1. What does it mean to "live up to your name"?

2. What are the three meanings of the name *Christian*?

3. What traits are associated with being Christlike?

4. How did the apostle Paul respond to the Galatians when they doubted him?

5. What does it mean to have commitment? Share a time when you made a commitment to someone.

6. In your own words, what does it mean to live with Christlike commitment?

7. What are some signs that a person is committed to Christ?

8. Do you think character and ethics have declined in the world? Explain.

9. How important is a person's character, and why?

10. Define *compassion,* and reflect on / discuss the connection between love and compassion.

11. Share a time when you were a giver or a receiver of compassion.

12. How are you going to become a more effective disciple of Jesus?

Activities

As a group: We are all disciples of Christ. Reflect on and then talk about how you see your particular role as a disciple. What spiritual gifts would you like to develop or use more often in service to God?

At home: Think about how you would rate your character right now. What changes would you like to make?

Prayer: *Dear God, we are your disciples. Help us show Christlike commitment, character, and compassion as we reach out to oth-*

ers. Open our eyes to the needs of others. Show us what needs to be done. Thank you for giving us everything we need to live as compassionate Christians. May we be sources of your love this week and always. Amen.

Chapter 5

Christlikeness in God

"Have No Regrets"

Snapshot Summary
1. Have no regrets regarding your compassion.
2. Have no regrets regarding your humility.
3. Have no regrets regarding your gratitude.

Reflection / Discussion Questions
1. What causes people to have regrets? Give an example.
2. Why are regrets a burden? How can they hinder your life?
3. Explain what it means to live in the spirit of Christ.
4. List some acts of compassion that people can perform today.
5. Give an example of how Jesus demonstrated compassion.
6. What causes people to lack compassion?
7. Share your definition of *humility*. Why is humility important?
8. Describe arrogant pride and explain why it is dangerous.
9. Why is humility scarce in today's world?
10. Why should Christians be grateful people? List ten reasons.
11. Name some ways in which we can express our gratefulness to God and to others.
12. How can a person live a life without regret?

Activities
As a group: Provide each person with materials to make a "Christlike: No Regrets" sign to display at their home or office, as a reminder of the lessons from this chapter.

At home: Take a pencil and paper and write down any regrets you have, then destroy the paper. Strive to live a life of no regrets.

Prayer: *Dear God, thank you for giving us the example of Jesus, who shows us how to live a life of compassion, humility, and gratitude. Help us get past our regrets and live for you and others today. May we be fearless about the future and learn from our past. Guide us this week and help us be loving people who live and act in faith. Amen.*

Chapter 6

Eternal Life in God

"What Do We Believe About Eternal Life?"

Snapshot Summary

1. Great Christians were not afraid of death, because they believed in eternal life.

2. Jesus taught us that because of the Resurrection, there is life after death.

3. The Bible's greatest promise is that God loves us, and God is with us on both sides of the grave.

Reflection / Discussion Questions

1. Reflect on / discuss some common fears people have about death.

2. According to the author, why do great Christians have no fear of death?

3. What are your thoughts about how the great Christians the author mentioned faced death?

4. How have your views on death and eternal life changed or remained consistent over time?

5. What did Jesus teach us about life after death? What is needed in order to gain eternal life?

6. Describe what you believe heaven is like.

7. List some ways in which we can prepare for death.

8. How can death influence how we live?

9. What roles do sorrow and sadness play when it comes to death?

10. What metaphor for death (for example, "Death is like passing through a doorway") do you find particularly helpful or comforting?
11. How does God offer comfort when death comes?
12. Why do you believe in eternal life?

Activities

As a group: Use Bibles to locate the promises of God. Make a list of those that are especially meaningful to you.

At home: Talk with a family member or friend and share your thoughts on death and eternal life in Jesus Christ. Meditate on God's promises of eternal life found in your Bible.

Prayer: *Dear God, you are with us on both sides of the grave, and we are so thankful for that. Help us remember your promises and live a life of no regrets. Show us what you want us to do. Help us take the time to pray and really listen to you and your Word. May we be of comfort to those who face death or are grieving the death of a loved one. May we use this life to prepare for the next. In Christ's name. Amen.*

Chapter 7

Sharing God with Children

"Train Up a Child"

Snapshot Summary
1. We can train up children to have a strong sense of commitment to Christ and his church.
2. We can train up children to have a strong sense of self-esteem.
3. We can train up children to have a strong sense of love and respect for other people.

Reflection / Discussion Questions
1. Share how parents or other adults in your life nurtured your faith as a child.

2. Share some early memories you may have of Sunday school or church.

3. Name some activities that help children learn about God and grow in their faith.

4. List some questions children may commonly ask about God.

5. Why is it important to pass along your faith and values to children?

6. How can you show children how important your faith is to you?

7. Explain why the best gift you can give children is Jesus Christ. How does this gift keep on giving?

8. List ways in which you can provide leadership to children within your church.

9. Share ideas on how to build strong self-esteem in children.

10. Complete this sentence: "Confidence comes from ... "

11. How can children learn to love and respect others?

12. How are you going to share God with children (today / this week)?

Activities

As a group: Explore the church library or a Christian bookstore to locate materials that would be helpful in sharing God with children.

At home: Reflect on someone who positively influenced your faith in God as a child or as a young adult. Thank that person—through a letter, phone call, or e-mail if possible, and/or by passing on that positive influence to a young person in your life.

Prayer: *Dear God, thank you for placing children in our lives. They are not only living treasures, but also our future. Help us nurture them in Christian faith and provide them with the love and self-esteem they need. Give us patience in our interactions with them, and help us see things through their eyes. May we be good role models for children and help them become mature and responsible Christians. Amen.*

Chapter 8

Finding God in the Bible

"How to Read and Understand the Bible"

Snapshot Summary

1. Some people approach the Bible allegorically or symbolically.
2. Some people approach the Bible literally.
3. Some people approach the Bible academically.
4. Some people approach the Bible personally.

Reflection / Discussion Questions

1. At approximately what age did you receive your first Bible? What was the occasion? What were your thoughts or feelings about this experience?
2. Name the benefits of reading the Bible on a daily basis.
3. Explain the author's statement: "When we read the Bible, we need to know what we are doing."
4. Reflect on / discuss the danger of interpreting the Bible allegorically.
5. What does the author mean when he says that there are no real literalists when it comes to interpreting the Bible?
6. What does the author mean when he talks about reading the Bible "in context"?
7. What are the benefits of the academic approach in reading the Bible?
8. Why, according to the author, is the academic approach to reading the Bible incomplete?
9. According to the author, what questions do we need to ask ourselves as we engage in a personal approach of reading the Bible?
10. What books of the Bible or individual passages of Scripture are among your favorites?
11. Do you have a particular translation (version) of the Bible you prefer? If so, what is it that you like about this translation?
12. What helps you read and understand the Bible? Share your ideas.

Activities

As a group: Use resources from your Sunday school classroom or your church library, or visit a bookstore, to compare and contrast different versions of the Bible. How many different versions can your group find?

At home: Reflect on your own approach to Bible reading.

Prayer: *Dear God, thank you for giving us the Bible, your Word, to be our guide in life. Help us read it daily, treasure it, and ably apply it to our lives. Open our eyes and minds as we read so that we may absorb your Word and gladly receive the lessons you would teach us. Bless us as we go forward serving you and others in the spirit of love. Amen.*

Chapter 9

Loyalty to God and the Church

"Hold On to the Church with Both Hands"

Snapshot Summary
1. We come to church with a gracious spirit.
2. We come to church with a strong witness.
3. We come to church with a deep commitment.

Reflection / Discussion Questions
1. Reflect on / discuss the importance of loyalty. Why is it often rare?
2. Share a time when you showed loyalty or when someone showed loyalty to you.
3. List some of the expectations you have when you arrive at church for worship services on Sunday or at other times during the week.
4. Explain what it means to have a gracious spirit.
5. How do you gain a gracious spirit?
6. What is meant by the statement "We can turn people on to the church or we can turn them out of the church by the way we treat them"?

7. Name some ways in which Christians can be a strong witness for God.

8. How can the words or acts of a strong witness touch the lives of others?

9. How does a person attain a deep commitment to church and to others?

10. What have you gained from your church attendance? How does regular, consistent attendance make a difference?

11. Name some of the signs that a person has a deep commitment to God and to others.

12. Reflect on / discuss some ways you can prepare yourself, before you leave home, for a meaningful worship experience.

Activities

As a group: Have each person create his or her own personal to-do checklist for preparing for worship services.

At home: Reflect upon what you give and what you receive when you attend church on Sunday and at other times throughout the week.

Prayer: *Dear God, thank you for the opportunity to worship you in church each Sunday and at other times during the week, as well as in our homes. Help us not take this freedom for granted. Guide our thoughts as we prepare to worship, so that we may receive full value from the experience. Show us how to share our faith with others, and encourage within us a deep commitment to you. Help us maintain our loyalty to you as we continue our faith journey. Amen.*

Chapter 10

New Life in God

"What Do You Want Me to Do Now?"

Snapshot Summary

1. God wants us to celebrate the gift of Jesus Christ.
2. God wants us to celebrate the gift of new vision.
3. God wants us to celebrate the gift of Christian friendship.

Reflection / Discussion Questions

1. When you come to know God, how does your life change?

2. How does God help you move forward and guide your actions?

3. Explain why *grace* and *Christ* were key words in Paul's conversion.

4. In your own words, what does it mean to celebrate?

5. Describe how it feels when you first receive the gift of Jesus Christ.

6. List ways in which you can celebrate the gift of Jesus on a daily basis.

7. Why is a fresh perspective or a new vision helpful in life? How do you get a fresh perspective?

8. How does knowing Jesus open your eyes and improve your spiritual vision?

9. Explain how Christian friendships are different from other friendships.

10. Why is a friendship a special gift?

11. List other gifts from God that we can celebrate.

12. If you desire to seek a new life in God, how do you begin?

Activities

As a group: Participate in Holy Communion together in celebration and gratitude for God's gift of new life in Jesus Christ.

At home: Place a colorful bow or ribbon on your Bible to remind you to celebrate God's gifts.

Prayer: *Dear God, thank you for the gift of new life you freely offer to each of us. Help us celebrate your goodness and mercy. May we share with others the gifts you give to us. Help us celebrate the gift of Christian friendship and treasure those with whom we share a faith in Jesus Christ. Grant us a new vision so that we may see the needs of others and be able to offer our help and love. In Jesus' name. Amen.*

Chapter 11

Commitment to God

"Be Careful What You Lean Your Weight On"

Snapshot Summary

1. We must be careful what we "lean on"—where we put our trust.
2. Lean your weight upon your family.
3. Lean your weight upon the church.
4. Lean your weight upon God.

Reflection / Discussion Questions

1. When you make a commitment, what are you saying?
2. List some of the commitments that God has made to us.
3. Why do we all need someone to lean on?
4. How do you know whether or not to trust someone?
5. Give some examples of where people wrongly place their trust.
6. Share a time when you correctly placed your trust in someone.
7. Explain why having a strong family is important to God and to our nation.
8. What values are learned within Christian families?
9. Name some of the ways in which the church can serve as your family.
10. How has the church helped you strengthen your commitment to Christ?
11. Reflect on / discuss some reasons why we can always rely upon the church.
12. Share a time when you leaned your weight upon God.

Activities

As a group: Give all participants a 3-by-5-inch card, and ask them to write on it the most important message they want to remember from this chapter. Share the messages. Ask class members to take their card home and to place it in a prominent place where they will see it often this week.

At home: Make a list of all the commitments you have made. Which need to be strengthened? Are you placing your trust where it should not be placed?

Prayer: *Dear God, thank you for your commitment to us and for all of the many blessings you have provided us. Thank you for our family and for the church. Help us treasure them and lean on them when we need support or direction. Remind us of the needs of others. Help us be there for them when they need someone to lean upon, and help us be worthy of that trust. Amen.*

Chapter 12

The Song of God

"God Gave the Song"

Snapshot Summary
1. We can keep the song—the good news of the Christian faith—alive with our attention.
2. We can keep the song alive with our understanding.
3. We can keep the song alive with our love.

Reflection / Discussion Questions
1. What is your favorite hymn or song of praise, and why is it special to you?
2. What lessons do we learn from Acts 3:1-10 through the words and deeds of Peter and Paul?
3. Explain what it means to "take up the song."
4. What special events in life can make us feel like singing?
5. What does the author say is our calling as Christians today?
6. Reflect on / discuss some times when people need our undivided attention.
7. List some things that divert our attention away from what is really important.
8. List some ideas for being a more understanding person.
9. Reflect on / discuss why understanding is so valued and so needed.

10. Why are the gifts of understanding and attention also considered to be gifts of love?

11. Name some ways in which we "keep the song alive" with love.

12. List ways in which music can enhance our life and spiritual development.

Activities

As a group: Give each person a hymnal and ask them to locate hymns that encourage attention, understanding, and love. Ask participants to share special phrases found in the hymns that reflect the song of God.

At home: Tie a string around your finger this week (or create some other prominent form of reminder) to remind yourself to be more attentive, understanding, and loving.

Prayer: *Dear God, thank you for the gift of song, which brightens our world. Guide us so that we keep the song alive in our hearts, in our words, and in our deeds. Help us freely give our attention to others, along with our understanding and compassion. Remind us of the power of love. Help us share it with others. Show us what needs to be done, and help us respond with a song in our hearts. Amen.*

Chapter 13

Bringing Others to God

"He Couldn't Keep Jesus to Himself"

Snapshot Summary

1. We can bring our brothers and our sisters to Christ.

2. We can bring our children to Christ.

3. We can bring all people to Christ.

Reflection / Discussion Questions

1. In your own words, explain what you discern to be the greatness of the disciple named Andrew.

2. Recall a time when you shared something you were excited about.

3. When you hear the phrase "bringing others to God," what thoughts or images come to mind?

4. How and why are all Christians missionaries or disciples for Christ?

5. What skills are necessary to have in order to tell other people about Jesus?

6. Once you know Jesus, why is it impossible to keep him to yourself?

7. Share your story of how you learned about Jesus.

8. What sometimes prevents Christians from sharing Jesus with others?

9. Name some of the ways in which children learn about Jesus.

10. What role can prayer play in bringing others to Christ?

11. Andrew shared Jesus with his brother. What lessons do we learn from this?

12. Name some simple ways in which you can bring others to Jesus.

Activities

As a group: Break into groups of two. Assuming the role of new acquaintances, take turns talking to each other about God.

At home: Search your Bible and other resources to explore the work of Christian missionaries, both historical and contemporary.

Prayer: *Dear God, thank you for the witness of Andrew and others like him. Help us be bold in our witness and share with excitement and enthusiasm the good news of Jesus Christ. Show us all how to be missionaries at home, at work, and at church. Open our eyes to new opportunities to share God's Word, and help us step out of our comfort zones to talk about our faith with others. Amen.*

Chapter 14

Marriage and God

"Celebrating the Gift of Marriage"

Snapshot Summary

1. If you want to have a happy, healthy marriage, don't be crabby; be grateful.

2. If you want to have a happy, healthy marriage, don't be critical; be respectful.

3. If you want to have a happy, healthy marriage, don't be controlling; be gracious.

Reflection / Discussion Questions

1. Name things that people often fail to understand about marriage.

2. What makes marriage worth all of the work that is required?

3. List some of the resources available to help improve a marriage.

4. Name a couple who inspire you in their marriage.

5. List some of the reasons why people get crabby.

6. How would you handle a spouse who is often crabby?

7. Reflect on / discuss why some people have a critical nature.

8. Why can constantly giving advice cause problems?

9. Reflect on / discuss the importance of mutual respect in a marriage.

10. How should decisions be made in a marriage? What are the dangers of being overly controlling?

11. List some ideas on how marriage partners can keep the courtship alive.

12. Name some ways in which you can make God a partner in your marriage.

Activities

As a group: Create a poster listing ten keys to a happy marriage. Ask every group member to contribute at least one idea. Display the poster on a wall or a bulletin board at church.

At home: Take your spouse out to dinner this week. If you are single and close friends with a married couple, you might offer to assist them with household chores in some way to enable them to have some free time to go out to dinner or a movie.

Prayer: *Dear God, thank you for the blessings of marriage. Help us treasure the relationships we have with others. Help us treat others with love and respect. Show us how to be both gracious and grateful. Open our eyes to opportunities to offer strength and support to those who are struggling in their relationships. And help us make you a partner in all of our relationships. Amen.*

Chapter 15

Purpose in God

"The Power of a Purpose"

Snapshot Summary

1. Purpose gives us the power to see problems as opportunities.
2. Purpose gives us the power to rise above the fear of criticism.
3. Purpose gives us the power to live meaningfully.
4. Purpose gives us the power to see the routine, mundane, and commonplace as sacred.

Reflection / Discussion Questions

1. What happens when people lack a purpose in life?
2. How does having a purpose give a person power?
3. Share a time when you turned a problem into an opportunity.
4. Does every life have a purpose? Explain.
5. What was Jesus' purpose?
6. Why do people fear criticism? How do you rise above it?
7. In your own words, what is a meaningful life?
8. List some keys to finding your purpose in life.
9. Do you think your purpose in life can change as you grow older? Explain your reasoning.

10. How do you learn God's purpose for your life? Can you have a purpose apart from God?

11. How can you help someone discover his or her purpose?

12. How have readings in this book, along with your reflections and discussions of the material, helped you in finding purpose?

Activities

As a group: Have a "graduation" party for the members of your study / discussion group. Create personalized completion certificates, then exchange them and write messages of gratitude and encouragement.

At home: Review this book and consider what you have gained by reading / studying it. Are there any changes you want to make in your life now?

Prayer: *Dear God, thank you for bringing this group together and for the sharing that has taken place. Thank you for the blessings of new friendships. Help us go forward with a purpose to our lives. May we gain the power that comes from purpose and use it to change lives and bring others to Jesus. Thank you for filling our hearts and our souls with your powerful presence, goodness, and love. Be with each member of our group as we go our separate ways, knowing that you are always with us and that you love us. Amen.*